PATENTS
COLORING BOOK

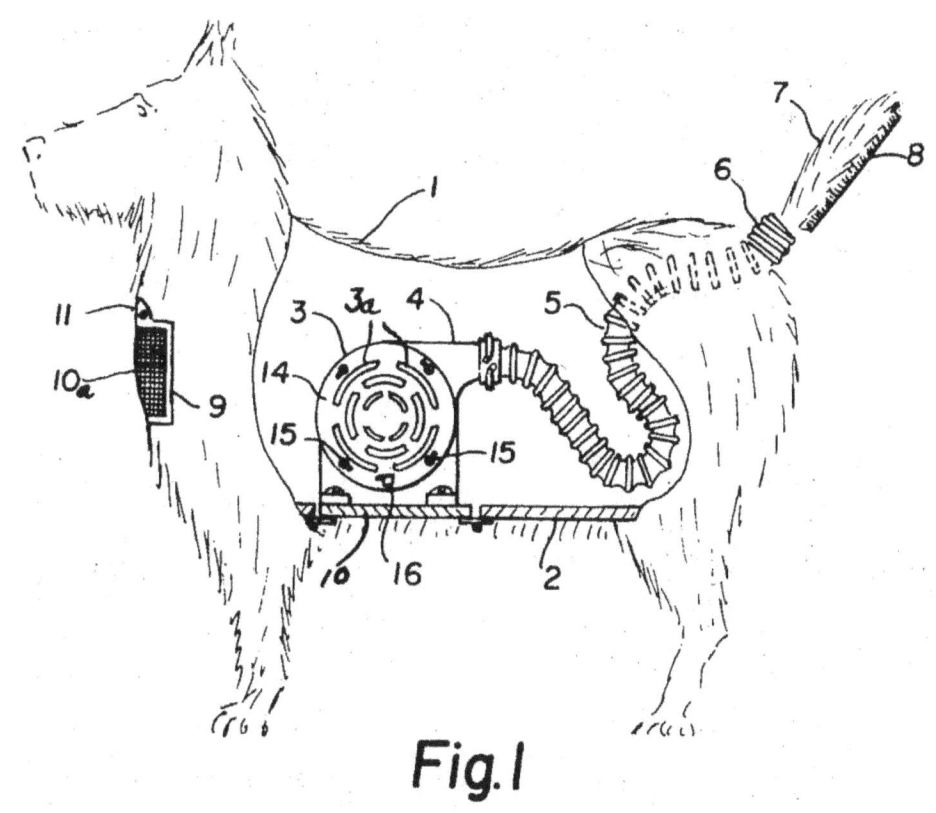

Fig.1

David Sorkin

ISBN 978-1-5196-7911-6

PATENTS COLORING BOOK

The illustrations and patent abstracts found on the odd-numbered pages of this book are all reproduced from patents published by the United States Patent and Trademark Office. Notations on the even-numbered pages are original except for material in quotation marks, which is taken directly from the published patents. Interested readers may find further information about the inventions depicted in this book at the Patent Office's website, www.uspto.gov, and on Google Patent Search, www.google.com/patents.

Richard Knerr and Arthur "Spud" Melin founded Wham-O Mfg. Co. in 1948. In addition to the hula hoop, Wham-O's products included the Frisbee flying disc, Silly String, the Slip 'N Slide, and the Super Ball.

Fig. 1.

Hoop toy

U.S. Patent number 3,079,728 (1963)
Inventor: Arthur K. Melin

The invention relates to toys and more particularly to toys in the form of a hoop for use about the body of a user. A preferred embodiment of the invention is a toy which comprises a tubular member formed into a rigid closed loop. The loop has a diameter larger than the widest dimension of the user of the toy. The weight and the diameter of the loop forming the hoop is proportioned so that the hoop may be caused to rotate about the body of a user for relatively long periods of time by co-ordinated movement of the body of the user.

Back when everyone bought their music on vinyl, the Discwasher record care system was the definitive method of keeping records free of dust and static.

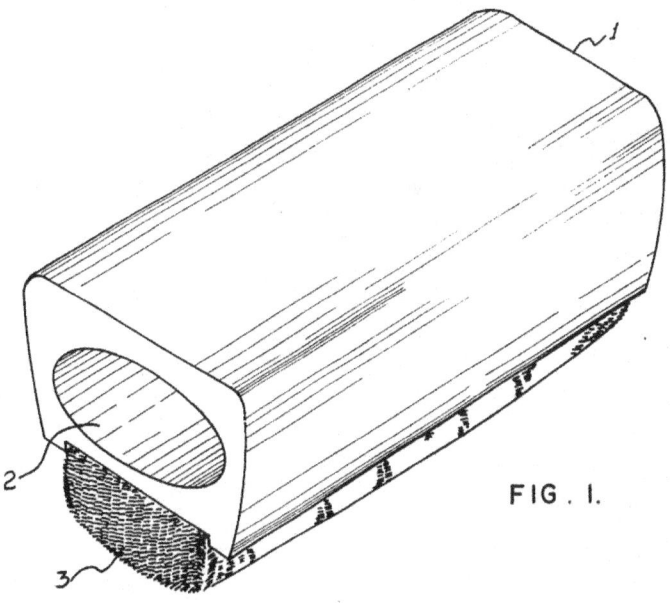

FIG. 1.

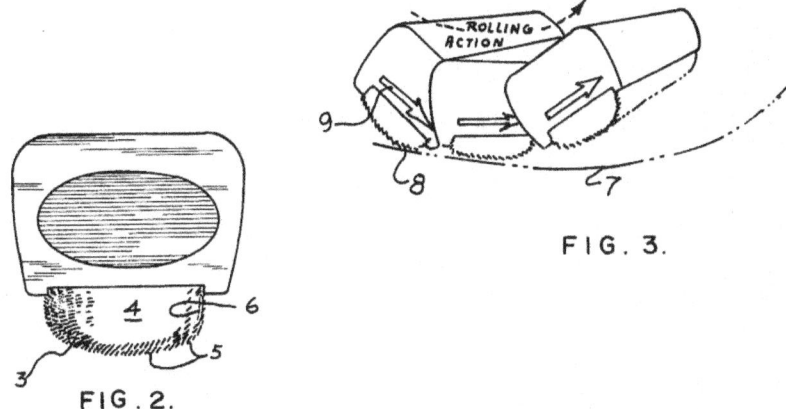

FIG. 2.

FIG. 3.

Phonograph record cleaning composition

U.S. Patent number 3,951,841 (1976)
Inventor: Bruce R. Maier

A cleaning composition of high chemical activity with anti-fungal properties, and with low dry weight residue and particularly useful for cleaning the surface of phonograph records; the mixture includes a surfactant, an emulsifier, an anti-microbe or fungicide, all intermixed in a liquid carrier such as water. This composition is most effective when used in combination with a brush designed having a cloth cover whose projecting filament form a pile that is finished and maintained angularly, and which when brushed against this pile effectively loosens dirt particles from the phonograph record surfaces being treated. In the method of use of this invention, the cleaning composition may be applied to the leading edge of said brush pile, with the brush then being moved simultaneously across and with a rolling action upon the surface being cleaned, as for example, the phonograph record surfaces, thereby effectively cleaning the disc of lipids, dust particles, and fungal particles that may clog and/or be germinating in the microgrooves of the same.

Douglas Engelbart's "X-Y position indicator" was the first computer mouse. The name was derived from the appearance of the device, whose cord resembled the tail of a mouse. Engelbart is also recognized for his work in developing hypertext, the concept on which the web is based.

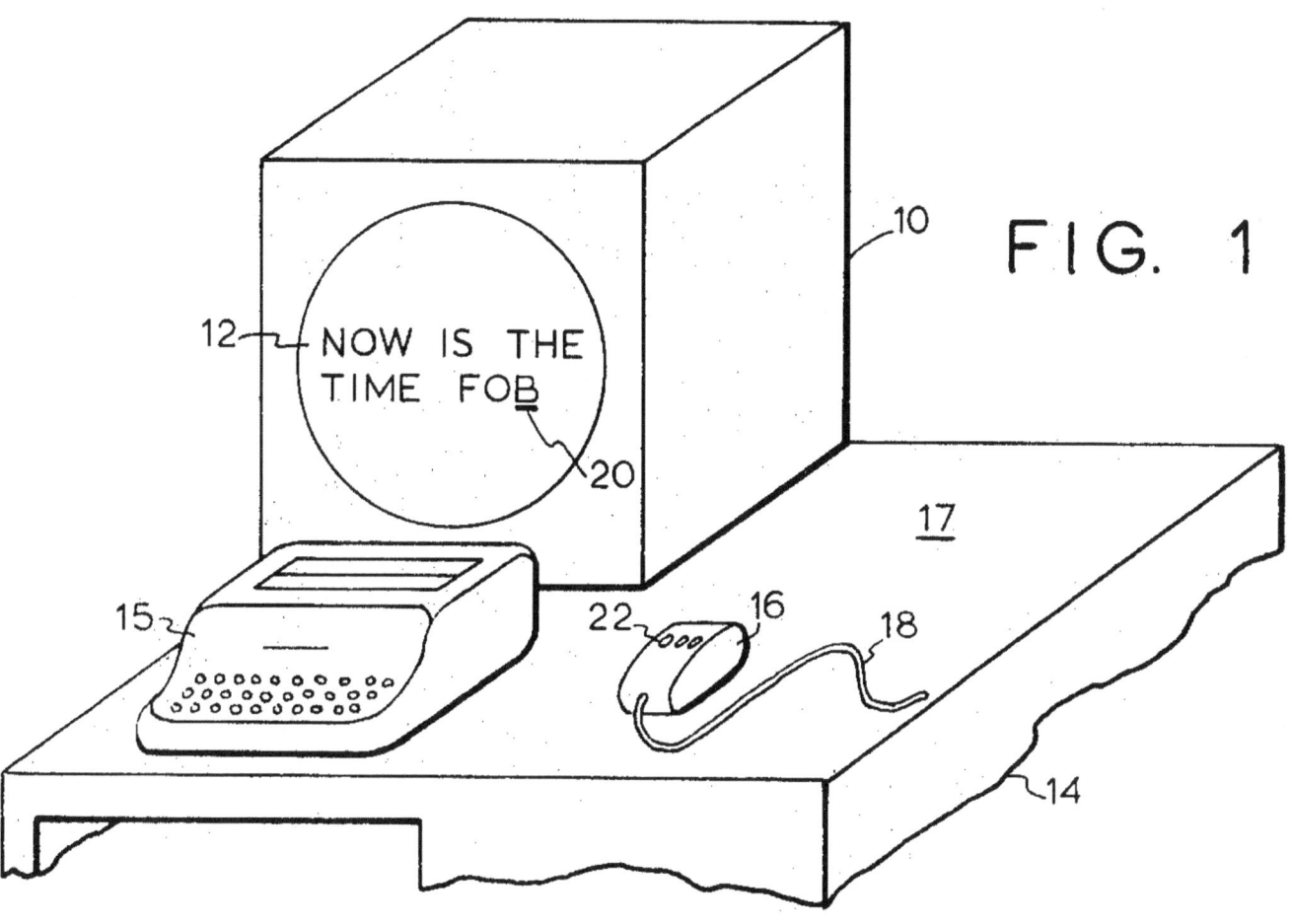

FIG. 1

X-Y position indicator for a display system

U.S. Patent number 3,541,541 (1970)
Inventor: Douglas C. Engelbart

An X-Y position indicator control for movement by the hand over any surface to move a cursor over the display on a cathode ray tube, the indicator control generating signals indicating its position to cause a cursor to be displayed on the tube at the corresponding position. The indicator control mechanism contains X and Y position wheels mounted perpendicular to each other, which rotate according to the X and Y movements of the mechanism, and which operate rheostats to send signals along a wire to a computer which controls the CRT display.

"The device is simple to use and enjoy. It provides vigorous body exercise in a game which requires no athletic skill, and which may be enjoyed by boys and girls alike in mixed play as a delightfully giddy and sometimes hilarious experience."

FIG. 1

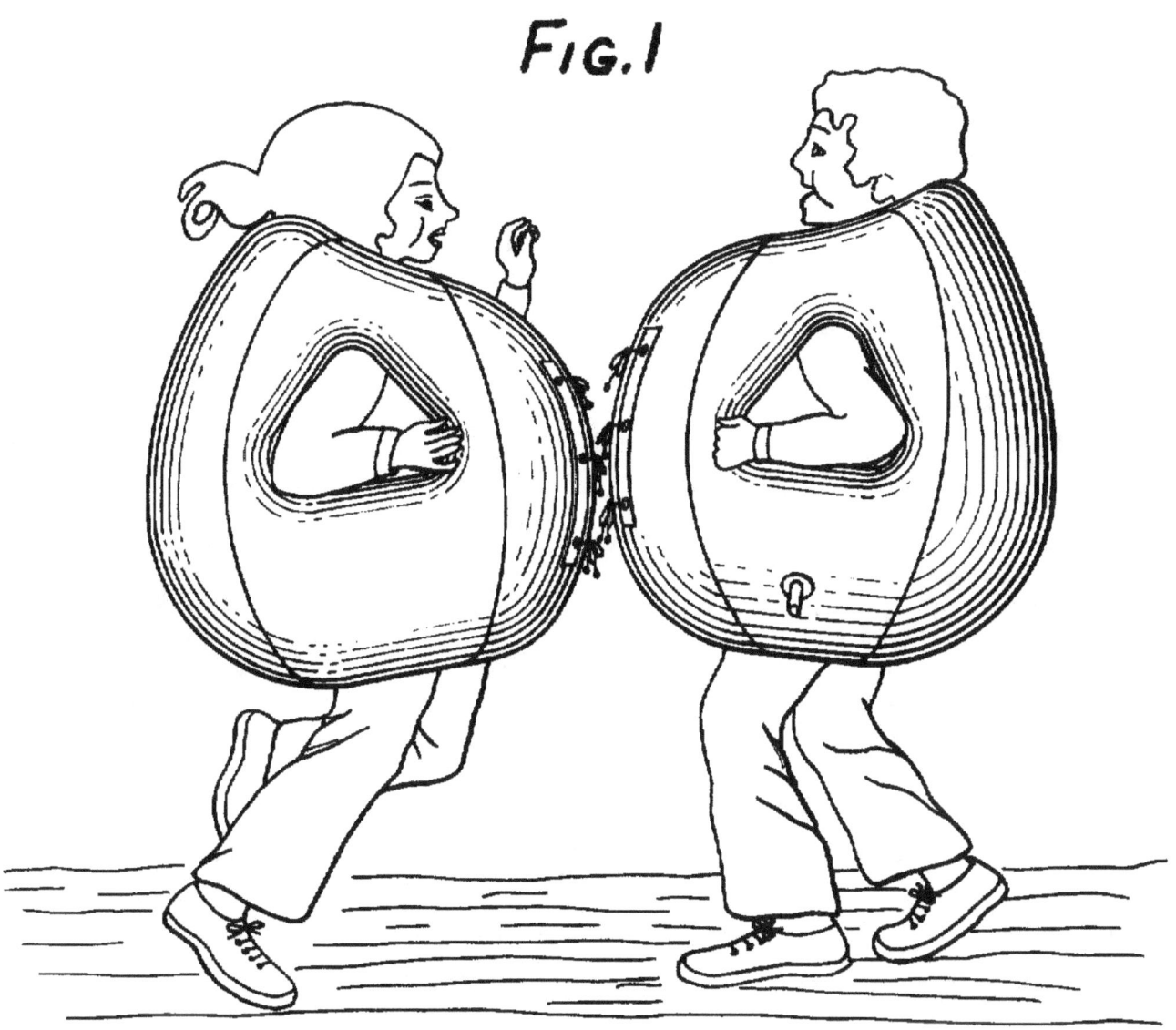

Inflatable body balloon

U.S. Patent number 3,972,526 (1976)
Inventor: James F. Cox, Jr.

A recreational and amusement toy for children in the form of an inflated balloon-like jacket which covers the torso, permitting children to bounce or roll off one another while standing erect or while prone upon a lawn or soft-surface play area. The generally spherical configuration permits the child to quickly return to his feet from either a bounce or roll action when balance cannot be maintained. Arms can be retracted with bent elbow into the arm openings to permit the child to roll readily on the ground.

Pringles inventor Fredric Baur died in 2008. At his request, some of his ashes were buried in a Pringles can.

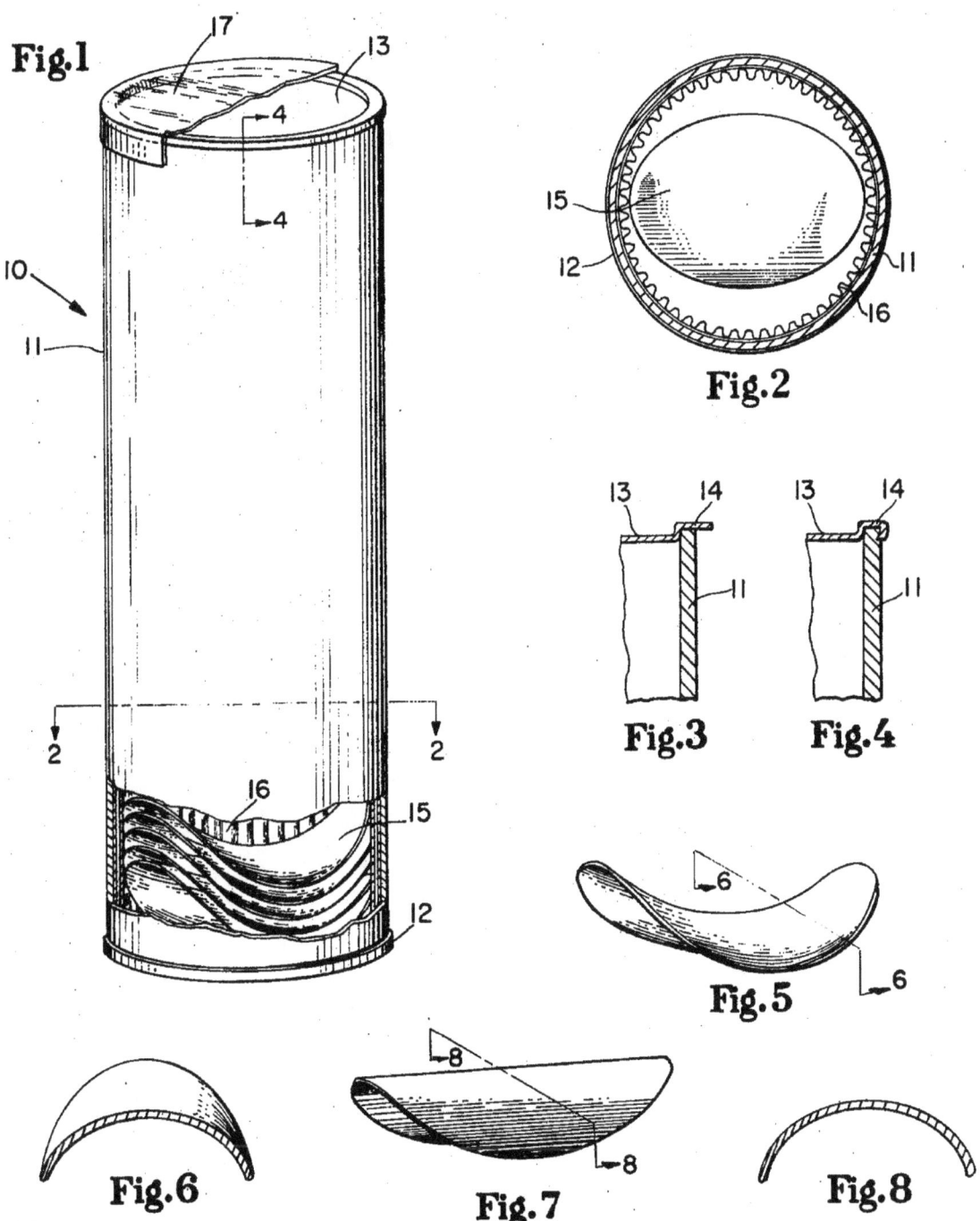

Packaging of chip-type snack food products

U.S. Patent number 3,498,798 (1970)
Inventors: Fredric J. Baur, Harold Kenneth Hawley

Chips of uniform size and shape are stacked one upon the other in closely fitting relationship to form a stacked array, and are then placed within a rigid tubular container formed from materials which are substantially impervious to the passage of oxygen and water vapor. The ends are applied to the container to seal the same.

Nintendo released the original Game Boy in 1989. Over 100 million units have been sold. In 2009 the Game Boy was inducted into the National Toy Hall of Fame.

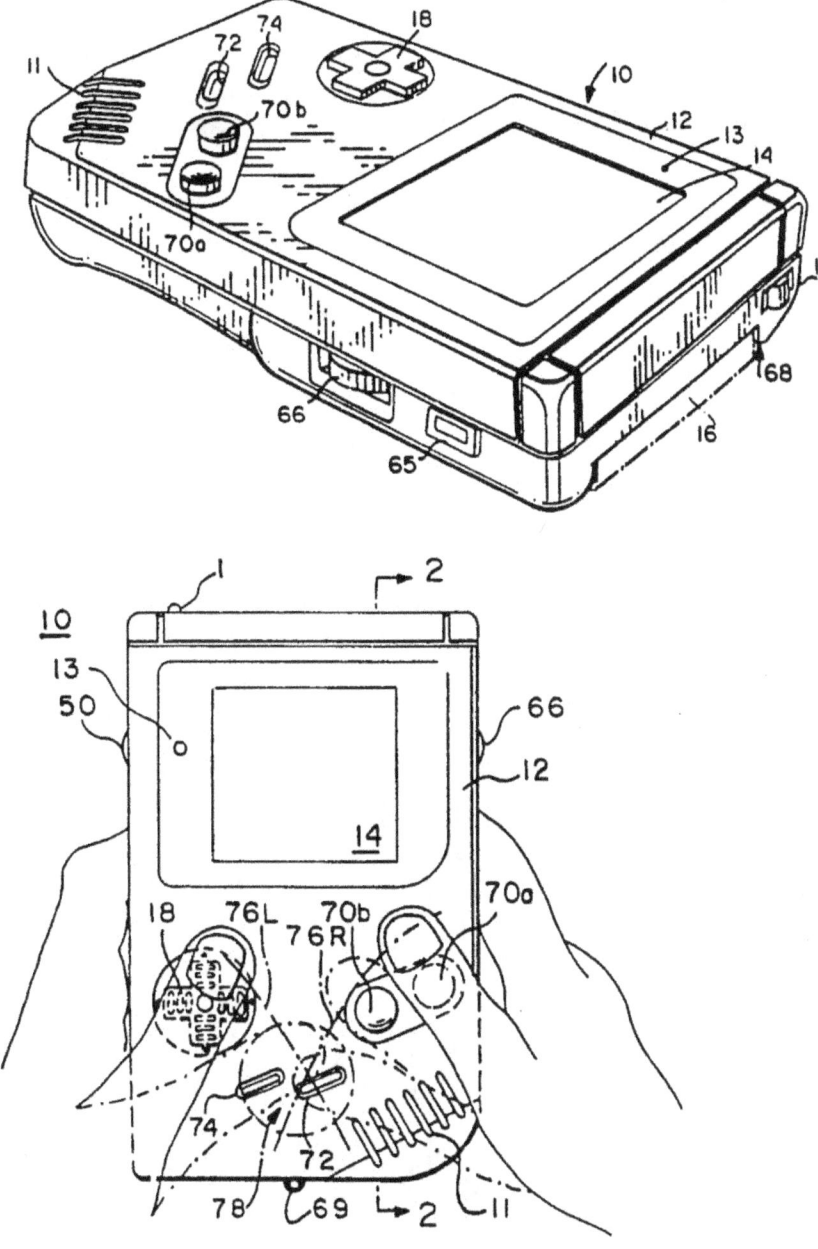

Compact hand-held video game system

U.S. Patent number 5,184,830 (1993)
Inventors: Satoru Okada, Shin Kojo

A hand-held electronic game machine for use with attachable/detachable memory game packs wherein the game machine includes a case of a size which may be held by a hand and capable of being sandwiched by both hands with a first switch disposed at a position such that during a game it can be operated by one thumb on a front surface of the case, a second switch disposed at a position such that during a game it can be operated by the other thumb on the first surface of the case and a third operation switch means provided in a region of said front surface where imaginary loci of both thumbs intersect with each other on the front surface, and wherein the game machine can be connected with others for simultaneous multiple player competition.

The can opener wasn't invented until many years after the can.

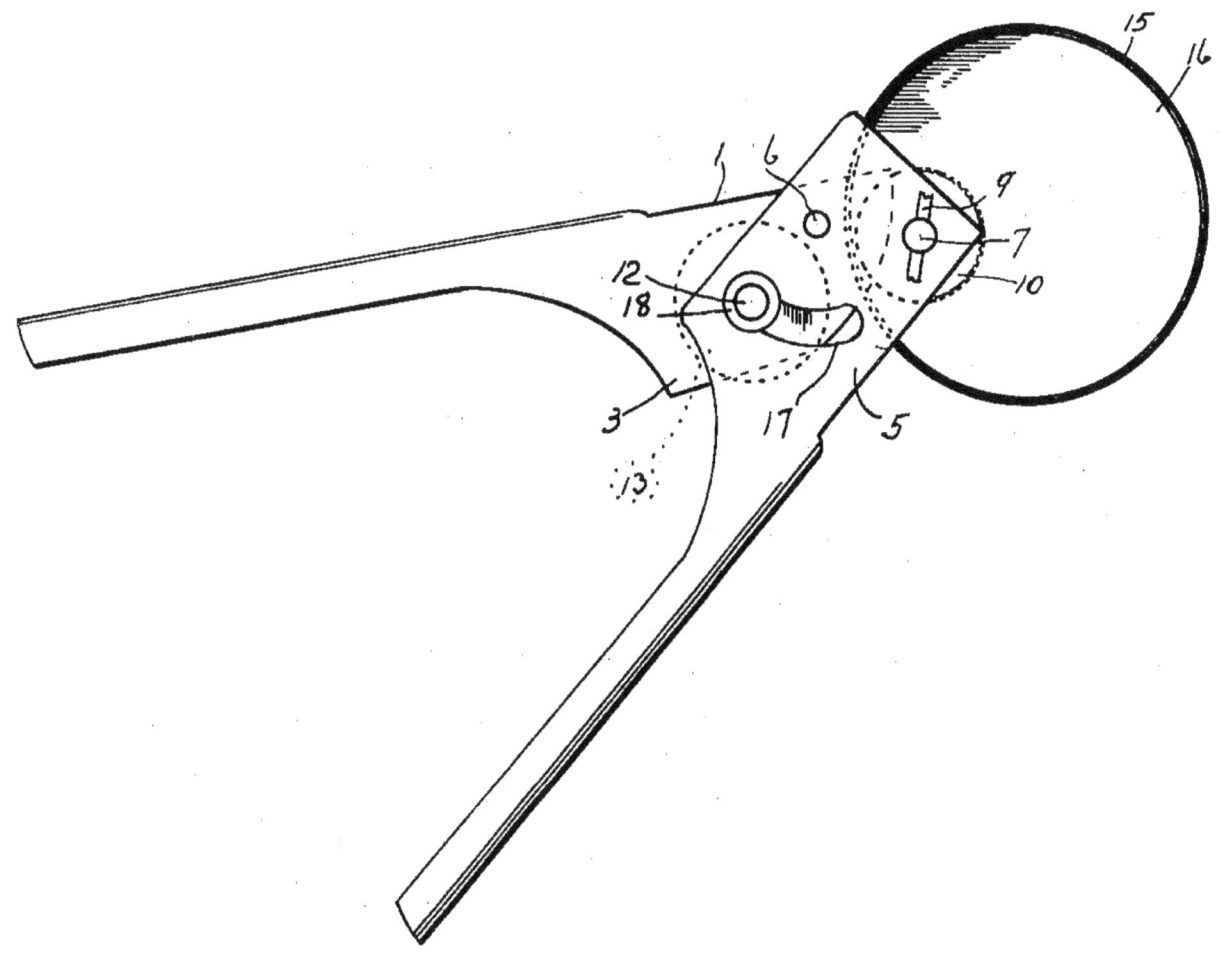

Can opener

U.S. Patent number 1,599,765 (1926)
Inventor: John E. Hoffman

My invention relates to can openers, and particularly to a device of this character adapted to sever the end of the can, and the object of the invention is to provide an inexpensive can opener having facility for severing the head of the can with a circular blade. A further object of the invention is to provide handles provided with pivotally connected telescoping heads, one of which is provided with a rotary blade and the other being provided with facilities to cooperate with the blade to sever the head of the can.

Best known as the lead guitarist of Van Halen, Eddie Van Halen is also an inventor, with three patents to his name.

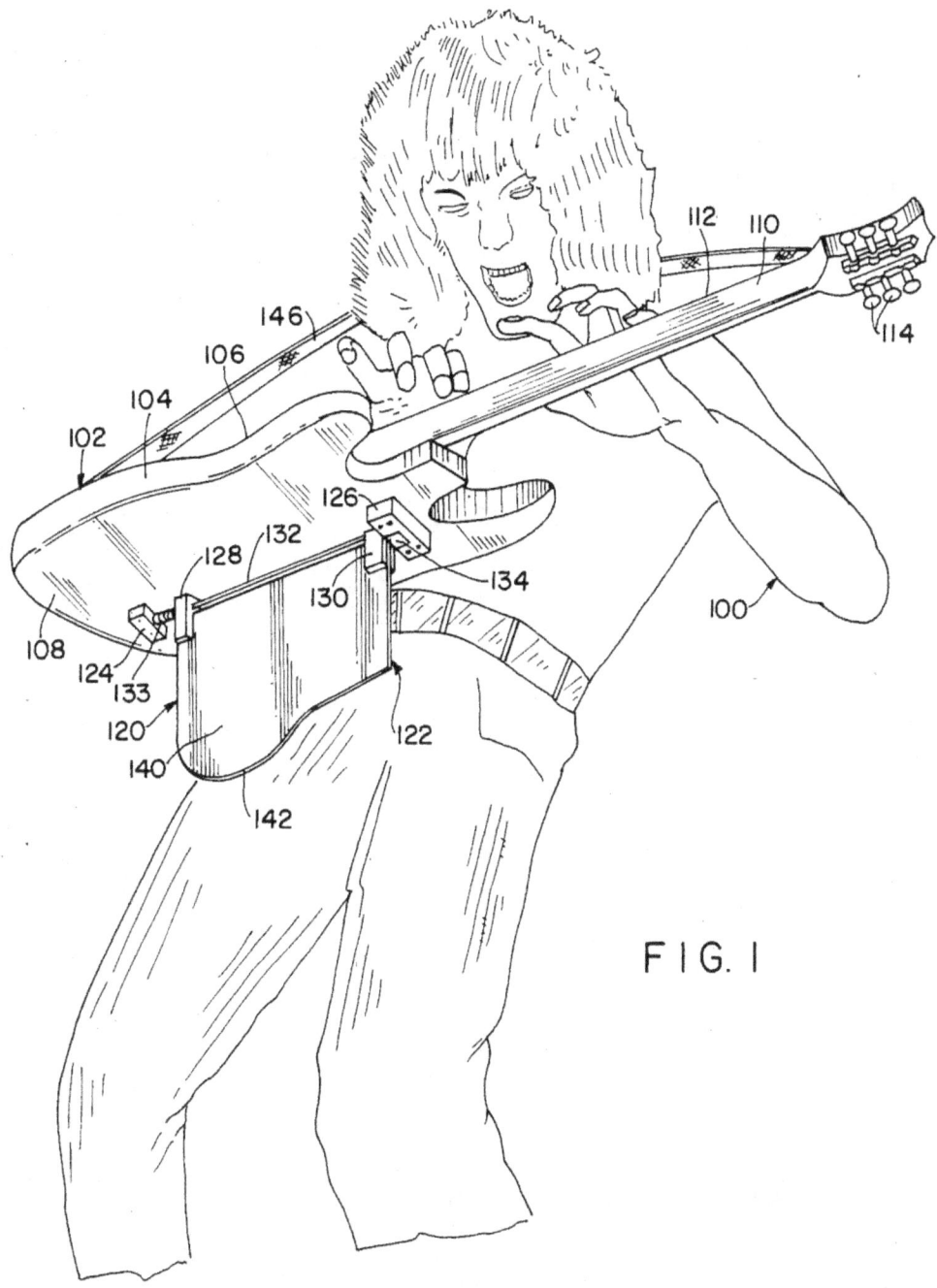

FIG. 1

Musical instrument support

U.S. Patent number 4,656,917 (1987)
Inventor: Edward L. Van Halen

A supporting device for stringed musical instruments, for example, guitars, banjos, mandolins and the like, is disclosed. The supporting device is constructed and arranged for supporting the musical instrument on the player to permit total freedom of the player's hands to play the instrument in a completely new way, thus allowing the player to create new techniques and sounds previously unknown to any player. The device, when in its operational position, has a plate which rests upon the player's leg leaving both hands free to explore the musical instrument as never before. Because the musical instrument is arranged perpendicular to the player's body, the player has maximum visibility of the instrument's entire playing surface.

"During a televised sporting event, a 'high five' is commonly shared between fans to express the joy and excitement of a touchdown, home run, game-winning basket, birdie or other positive occurrence. Unfortunately, as known in the art, a 'high five' requires the mutual hand slapping of two participants, wherein a first participant slaps an upraised hand against the elevated hand of a second participant. As such, a solitary fan is unable to perform a 'high five' to express excitement during a televised sporting event. In order to avoid the disadvantages of the prior art, the present invention provides a pivotable, self-righting hand-arm configuration for simulating a 'high five' when struck by the hand of a user."

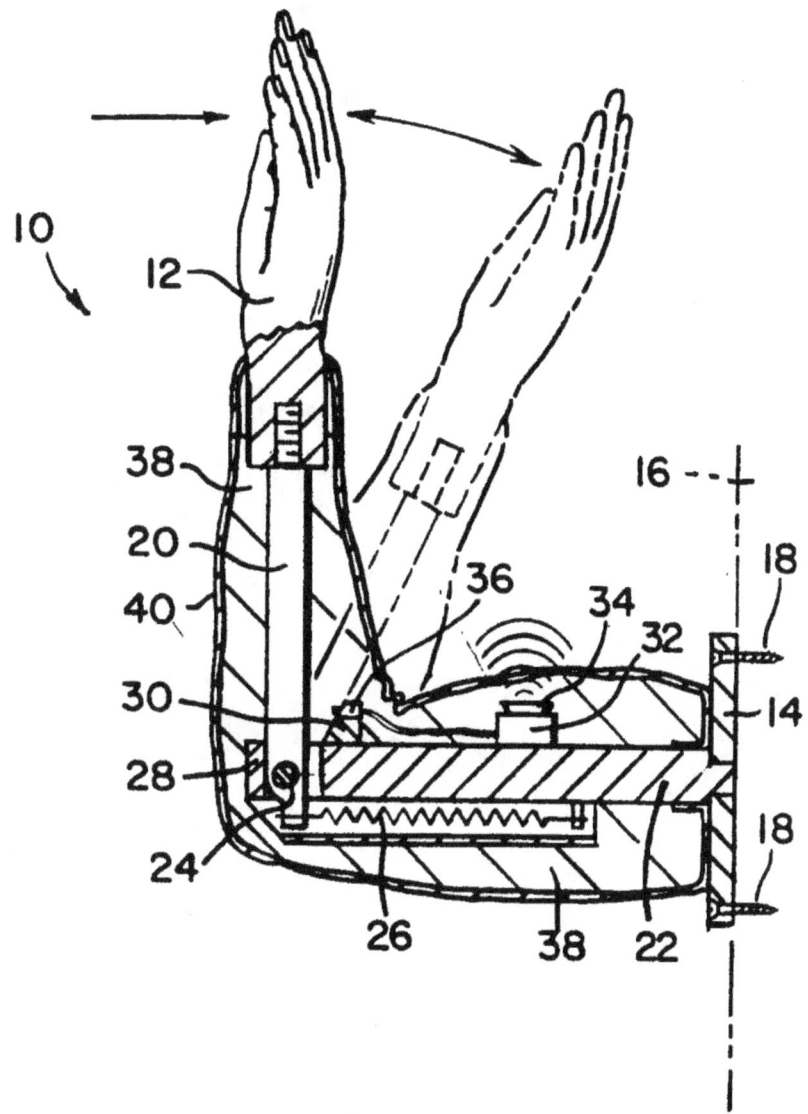

Apparatus for simulating a "high five"

U.S. Patent number 5,356,330 (1994)
Inventor: Albert Cohen

An apparatus for simulating a "high-five" including a lower arm portion having a simulated hand removably attached thereto, an upper arm portion, an elbow joint for pivotally securing the lower arm portion to the upper arm portion, and a spring biasing element for biasing the upper and lower arm portions towards a predetermined alignment.

Legend has it that the inventors of Silly String offered their invention to Wham-O but were initially rebuffed after spraying their concoction all over the executive's office. When the company's owners saw a stray piece of Silly String the next day, however, Wham-O hastily offered the inventors a contract for what ultimately became the largest-selling novelty toy in the world.

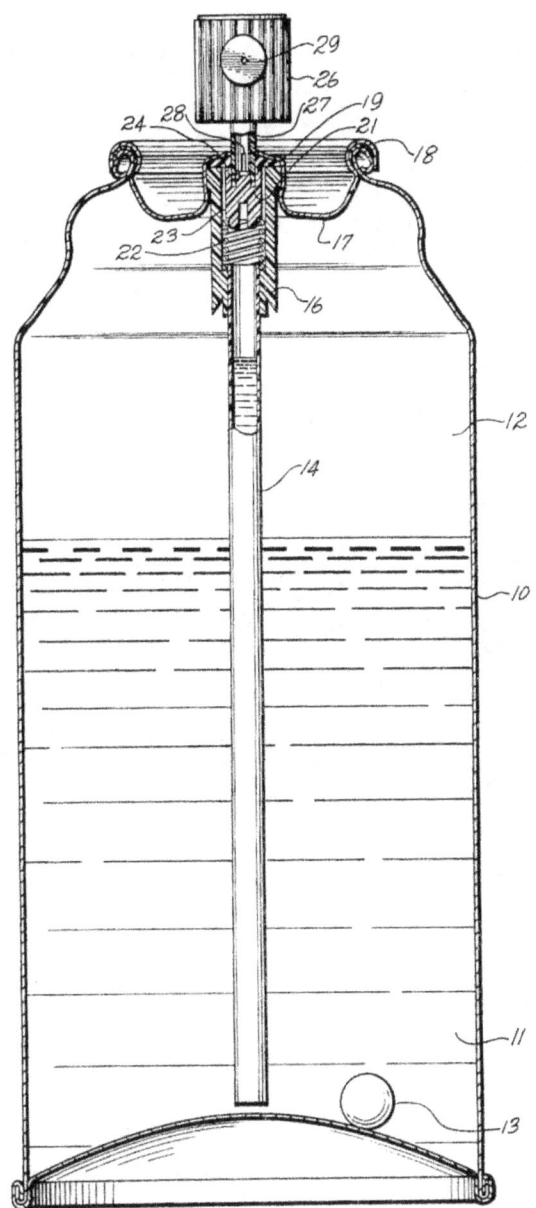

Foamable resinous composition

U.S. Patent number 3,705,669 (1972)
Inventors: Robert P. Cox, Leonard A. Fish

A pressurized or "aerosol" can containing a composition of matter for producing a string of plastic foam is described. The plastic foam produced from the aerosol can is in the form of a cohesive plastic body sufficiently tacky to adhere to inert surfaces such as walls, windows or the like to support the weight of the foam, however, of insufficient tackiness to adhere with a force greater than the cohesive strength of the foam so that the foamed body can be readily removed from surfaces to which it lightly adheres. Such a combination has substantial play and decorative utility.

"Pet birds comprise a special class of domesticated animals whose ability to fly and walk pose unique sanitary problems. In the past, the increased degrees of freedom associated with pet birds have warranted caging them for sanitary and protective reasons. However, keeping a pet bird in a cage, while allowing for the containment of excrement, severely limits the pleasure inherent in pet ownership."

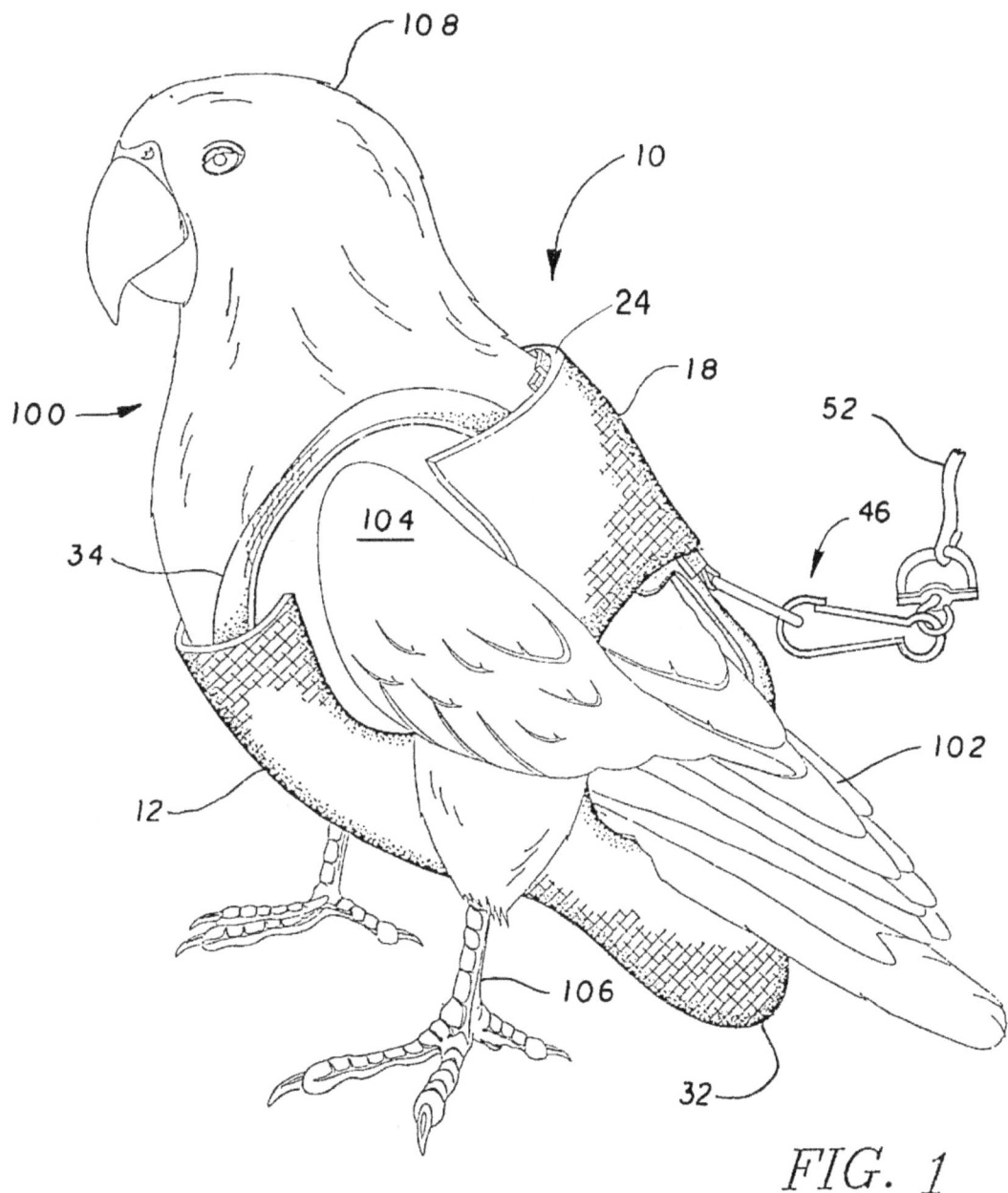

FIG. 1

Bird diaper

U.S. Patent number 5,934,226 (1999)
Inventors: Lorraine Moore, Mark Moore, Cely Giron

A bird diaper for an uncaged pet bird to wear, featuring an enclosed pouch for receiving and containing excrement, and apertures to accommodate both the wings and the tail of the bird. Elastic straps and hook and loop fastener components (e.g., VELCRO) secure the diaper onto the body of the pet bird without restricting movement. The bird diaper is fabricated from spandex (e.g., LYCRA) or another stretchable, lightweight material, allowing absorption of bird excrement to prevent leaks and facilitating easy cleaning using soap and water. The bird diaper can incorporate decorative designs, bright colors and is available in different sizes. The bird diaper also has a leash which is insertable within the hook and loop fasteners. The leash serves to restrain or limit the bird's area of free flight.

NASA tried to develop a pen that would write in space, but gave up in the face of soaring development costs. Once the Fisher pen was available, however, NASA and the Soviets began purchasing pens for their missions.

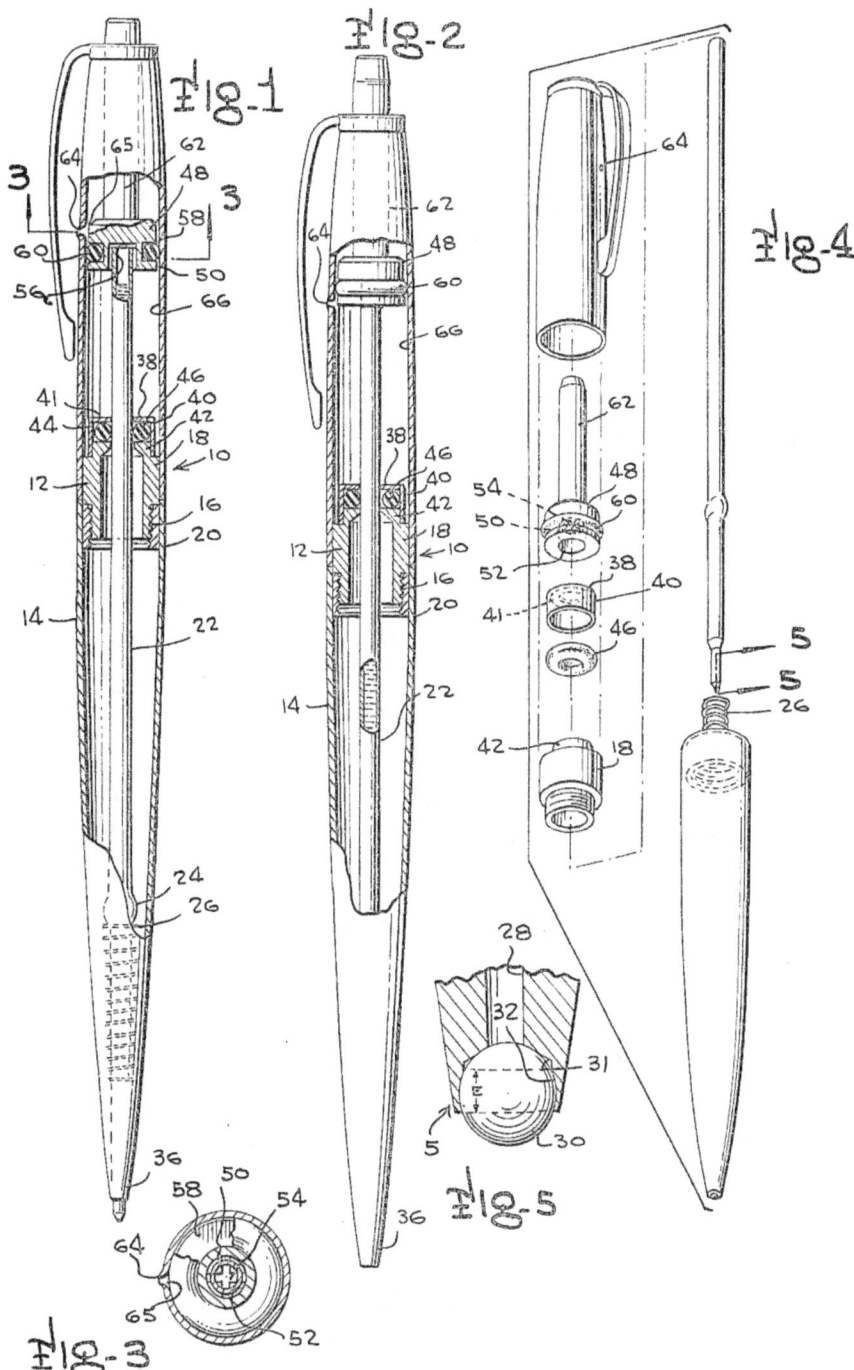

Anti-gravity pen

U.S. Patent number 3,285,228 (1966)
Inventor: Paul C. Fisher

This invention relates generally to pressurized ball point pens; more particularly, the present invention relates to ball point pens which may be used with the ball point in an elevated position relative to the ink supply. It is the principal object of the present invention to provide a ball point pen having a pressurized ink supply which enables the pen to write when the force of gravity acts against the flow of ink in the ink cartridge.

Apparently bike sails are a thing.

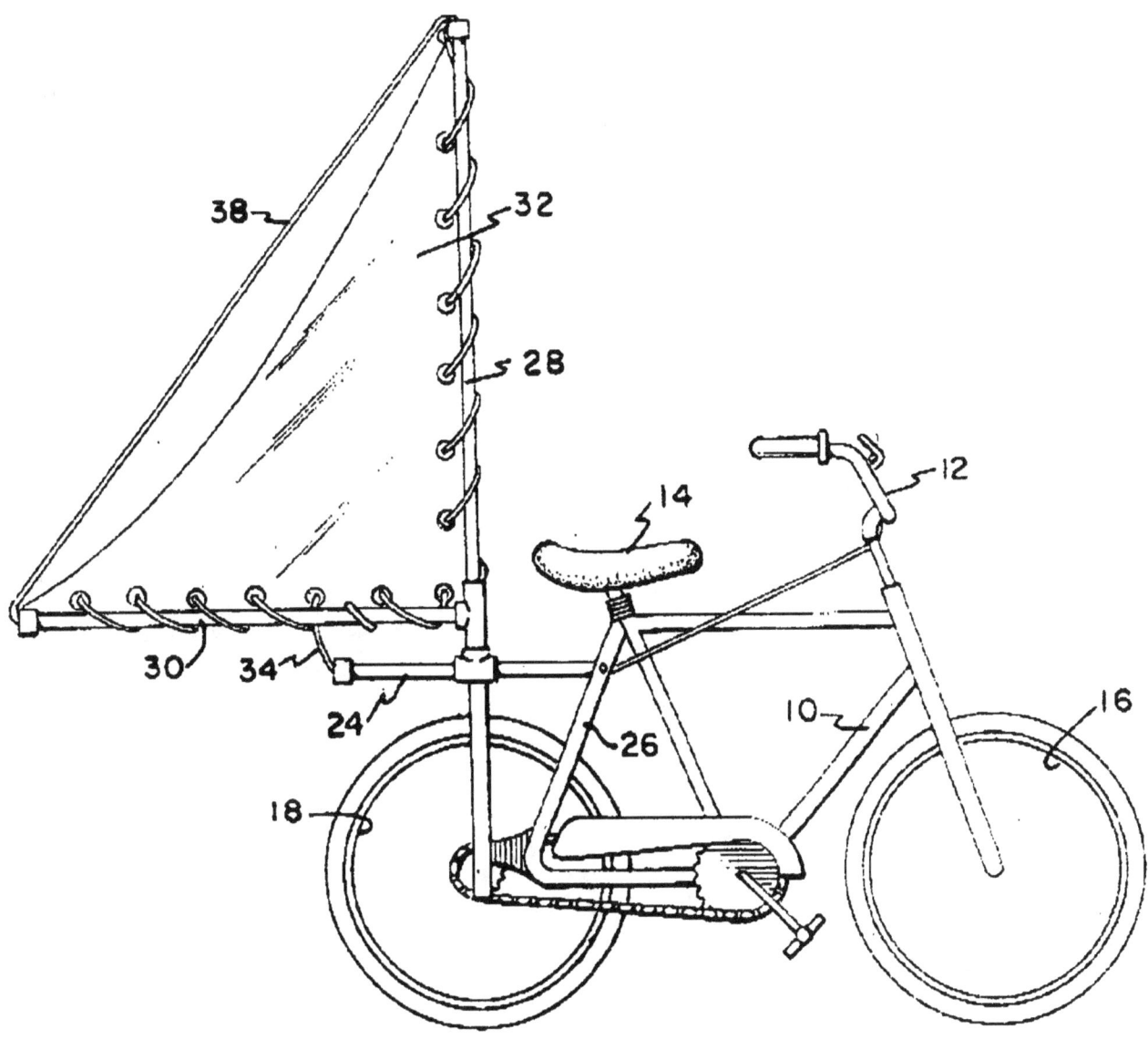

Apparatus for harnessing wind to drive a bicycle

U.S. Patent number 6,932,368 (2005)
Inventor: Vladimir Zam

A sail attachment which when connected to the bicycle harnesses wind to drive the bicycle forward. The attachment is adapted to fit on the rear of the bicycle above its rear wheel and is securable to the bicycle seat. The attachment is provided with a wind receiving sail which when attached to the bicycle can harness wind 45 degrees from either the left or right side of the bicycle, 90 degrees from either the side of the bicycle and at the rear of the bicycle to power the bicycle.

What child wouldn't want a dog that doubles as a vacuum cleaner?

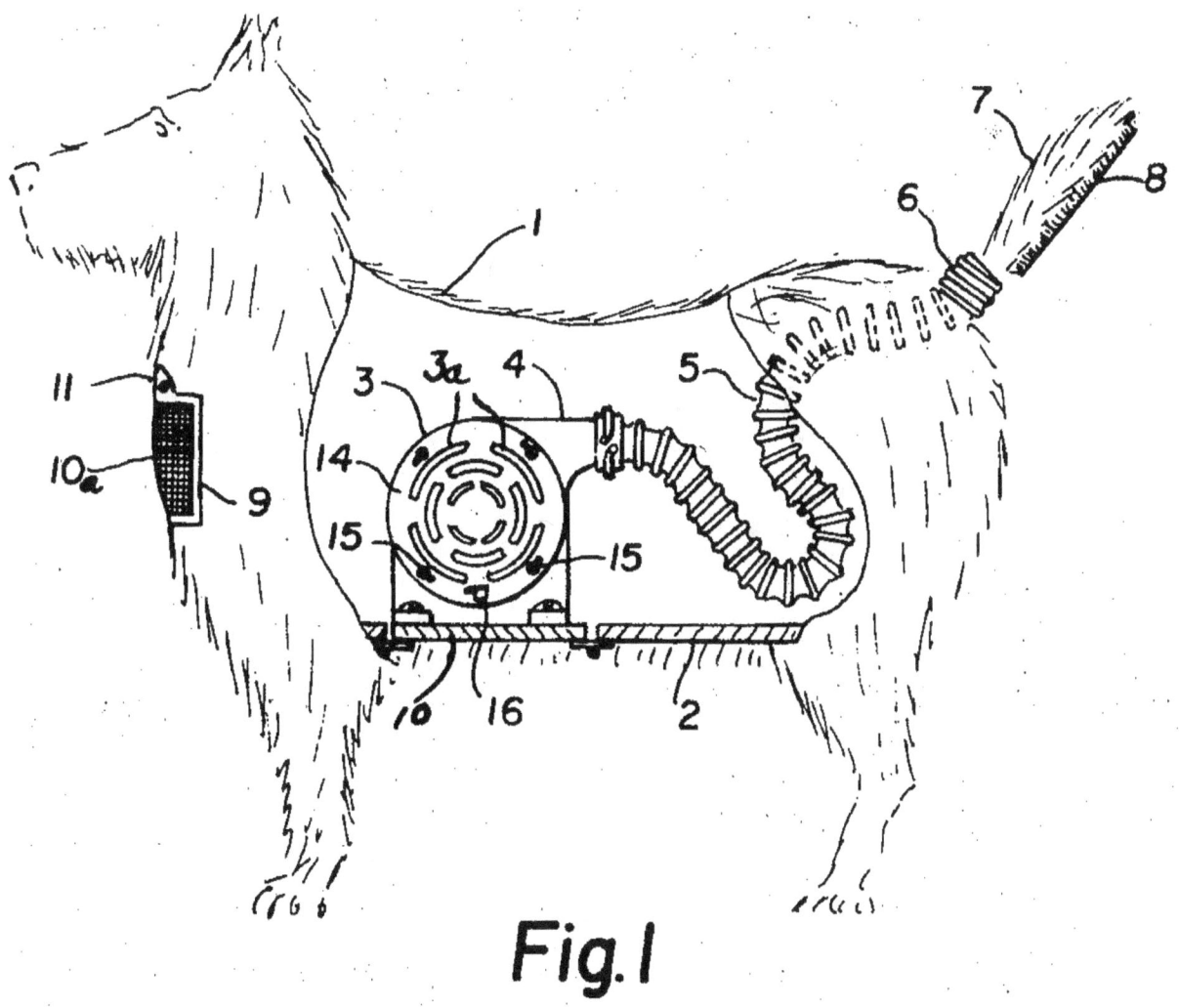

Fig.1

Combination toy dog and vacuum cleaner

U.S. Patent number 3,771,192 (1973)
Inventor: A. Zaleski

A toy dog closely resembling a real dog and having a hollow interior in which is mounted a vacuum cleaner having a suction hose which is retractable from the tail end of the dog. This enables vacuuming a dog after a hair cut and grooming without causing fear to the dog, inasmuch as the vacuum cleaner noise is greatly muffed by such enclosure. The vacuum cleaner is convertible to a blower and air issuing from the tail end can be heated so as to serve as a dryer.

William Alsbrook, a former fighter pilot with the Tuskegee Airmen, invented the salad sandwich with a removable plastic pouch to keep sandwiches fresh longer and potentially to make safe and nutritious food available during natural disasters. Students at The John Marshall Law School's Patent Clinic helped Alsbrook obtain his patent.

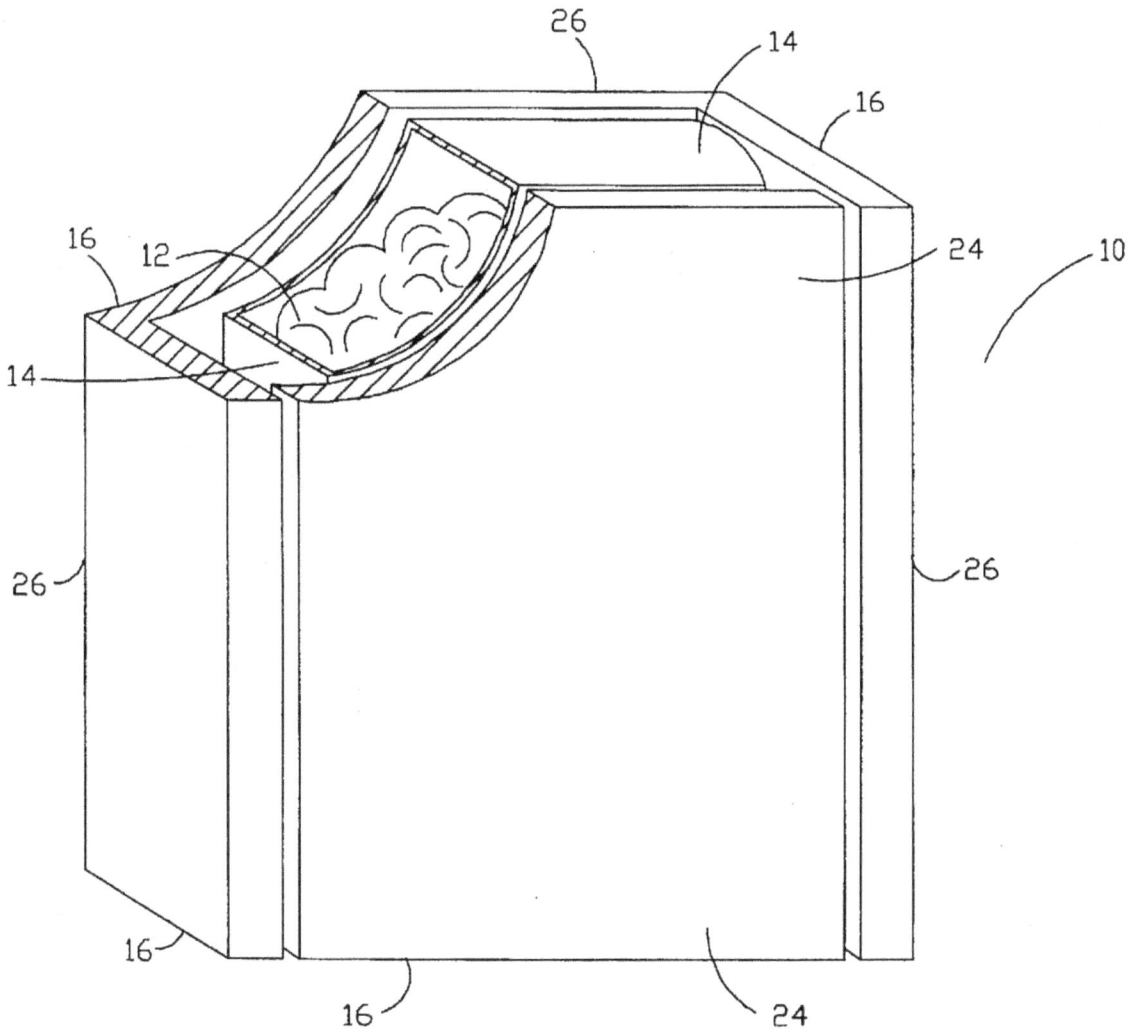

Salad sandwich and method of making

U.S. Patent number 5,567,455 (1996)
Inventor: William N. Alsbrook, Sr.

The invention comprises a salad sandwich and method of making the same where the salad sandwich is made of a baked edible shell that is open at one end and contains a tear-away bag which is filled with an appropriate sandwich fill. The tear-away bag keeps the sandwich fill fresh and prevents the sandwich fill from transferring moisture to the shell. The tear-away bag has a tear-away mechanism which, just before the salad sandwich is eaten, allows the bag to be removed in one step without removing the sandwich fill from the confines of the shell.

Yes, this one is real. Look it up if you don't believe me.

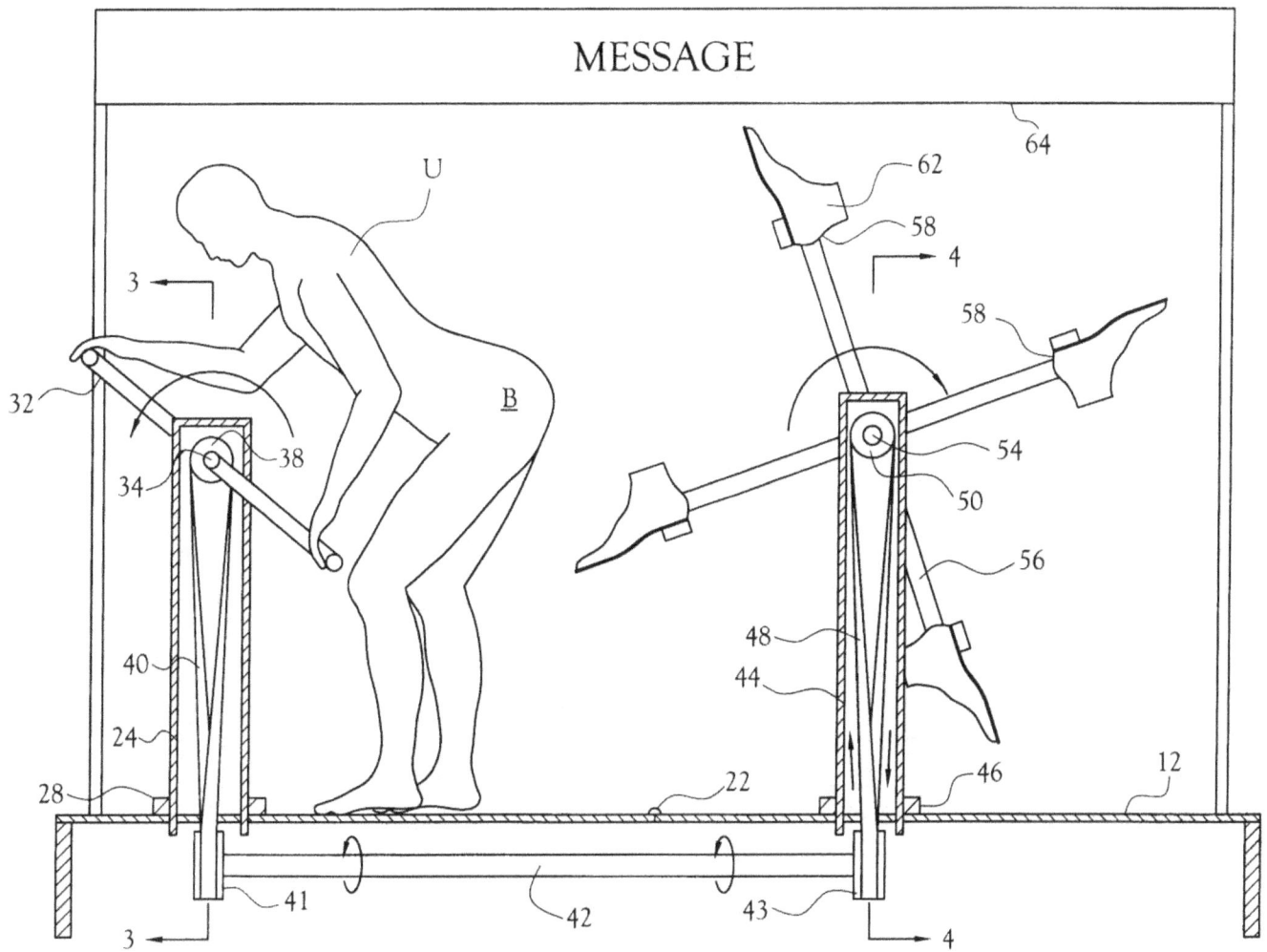

User-operated amusement apparatus for kicking the user's buttocks

U.S. Patent number 6,293,874 (2001)
Inventor: Joe W. Armstrong

An amusement apparatus including a user-operated and controlled apparatus for self-infliction of repetitive blows to the user's buttocks by a plurality of elongated arms bearing flexible extensions that rotate under the user's control. The apparatus includes a platform foldable at a mid-section, having first post and second upstanding posts detachably mounted thereon. The first post is provided with a crank positioned at a height thereon which requires the user to bend forward toward the first post while grasping the crank with both hands, to prominently present his buttocks toward the second post. The second post is provided with a plurality of rotating arms detachably mounted thereon, with a central axis of the rotating arms positioned at a height generally level with the user's buttocks. The elongated arms are propelled by the user's movement of the crank, which is operatively connected by a drive train to the central axis of the rotating arms. As the user rotates the crank, the user's buttocks are paddled by flexible shoes located on each outboard end of the elongated arms to provide amusement to the user and viewers of the paddling. The amusement apparatus is foldable into a self-contained package for storage or shipping.

In the 1920s and 1930s, it was apparently quite common to use monkeys as jockeys in greyhound races.

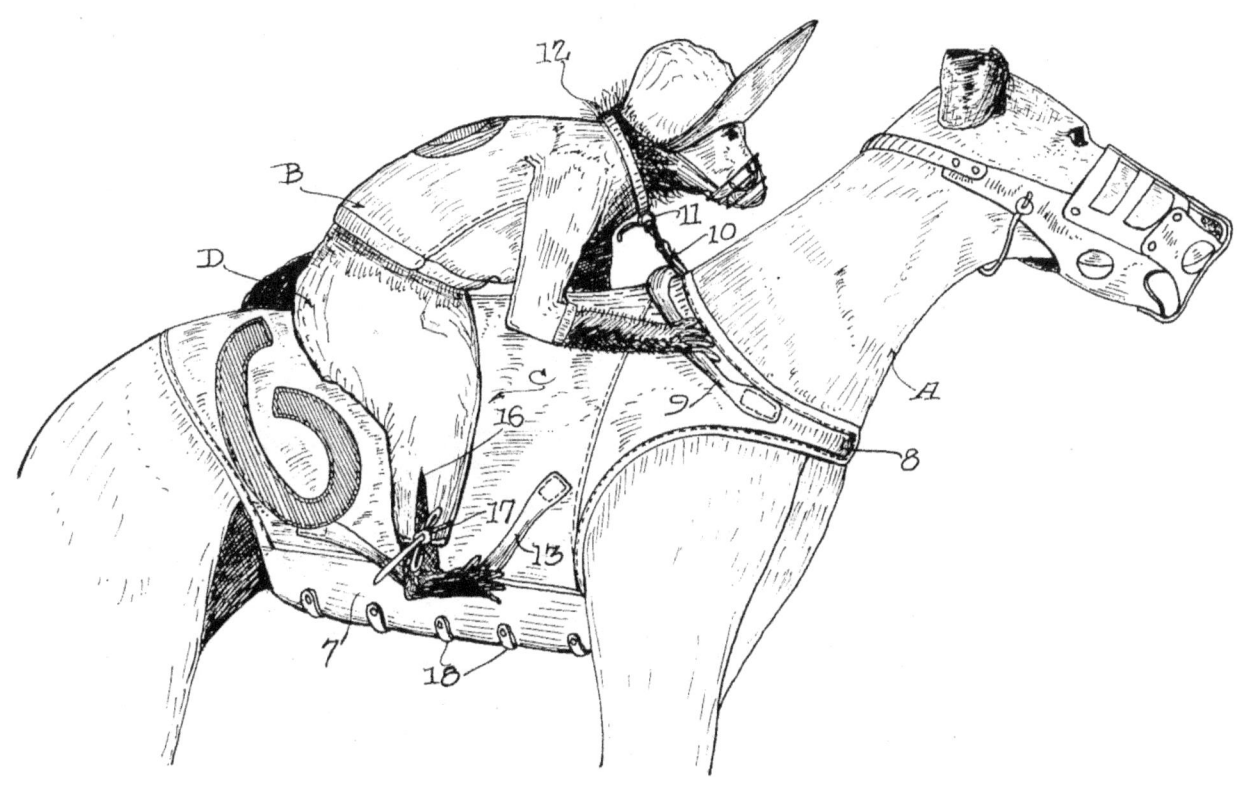

Combined racing greyhound harness and rider supporting means

U.S. Patent number 1,926,420 (1933)
Inventor: Rennie Renfro

This invention relates to improvements in harness constructions and has particular reference to a combined racing greyhound harness and rider supporting means. In the sport of greyhound racing, that is enjoyed by dog fanciers and racing enthusiasts, there has been recently introduced, the use of monkey riders, who serve in the capacity of jockeys. The principal object of the invention is to provide a novel and unique harness construction that will provide a comfortable dog fitting apparatus and a cooperating rider support that will safely retain the jockey in position on the back of the greyhound.

It's easier to get a patent than to defend one.

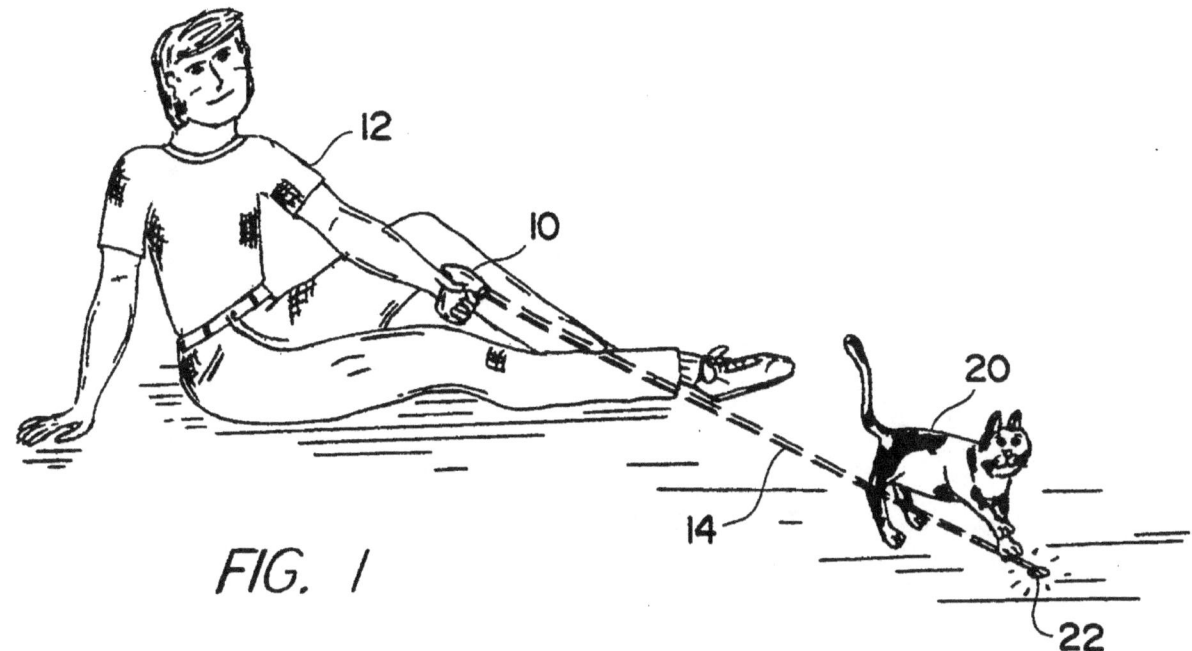

FIG. 1

Method of exercising a cat

U.S. Patent number 5,443,036 (1995)
Inventors: Kevin T. Amiss, Martin H. Abbott

A method for inducing cats to exercise consists of directing a beam of invisible light produced by a hand-held laser apparatus onto the floor or wall or other opaque surface in the vicinity of the cat, then moving the laser so as to cause the bright pattern of light to move in an irregular way fascinating to cats, and to any other animal with a chase instinct.

Lego began as a manufacturer of wooden toys in the 1930s, and soon branched out into plastic toys. The company developed the modern plastic brick design in 1958. Lego added minifigures to its line in 1978.

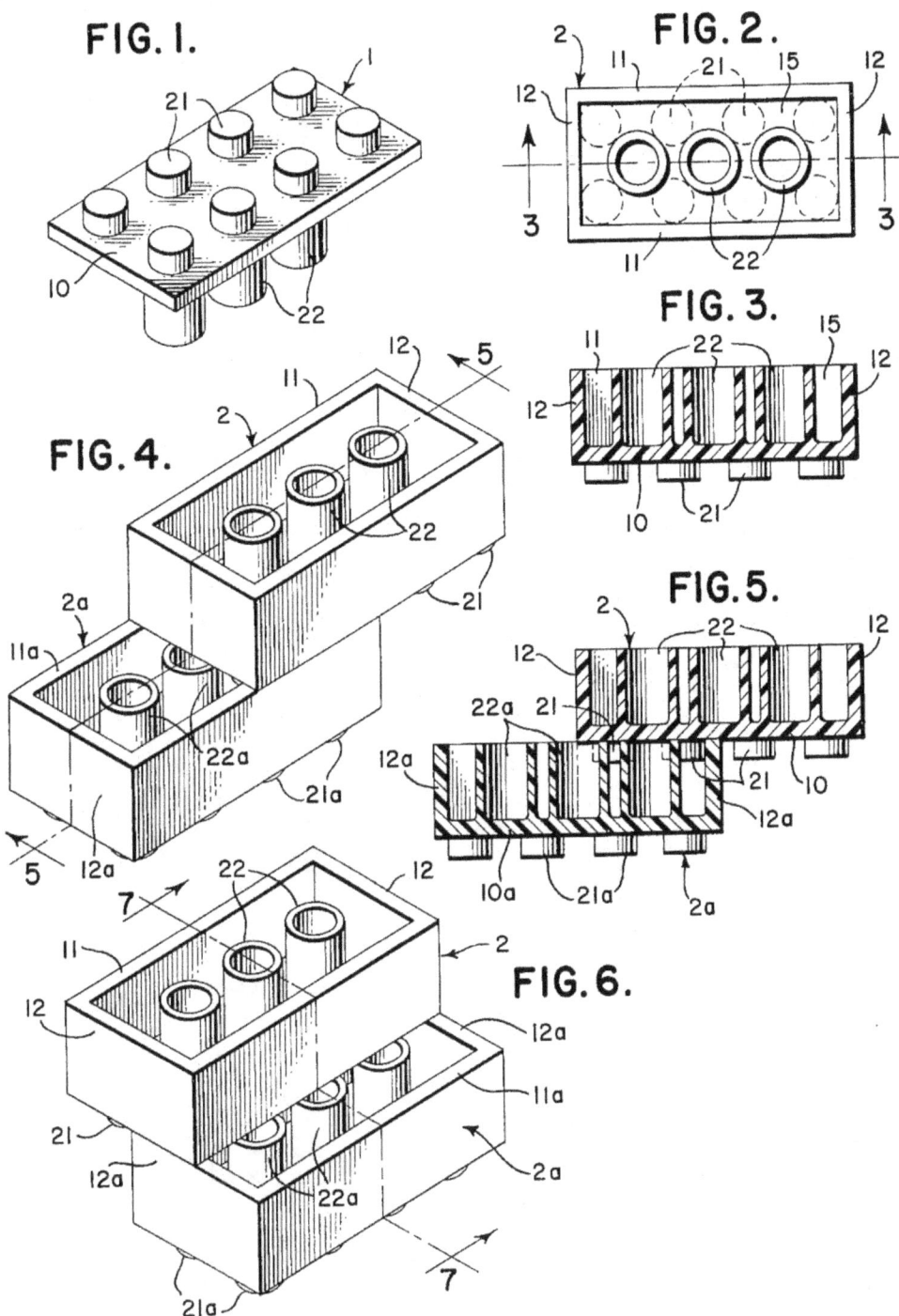

Toy building brick

U.S. Patent number 3,005,282 (1961)
Inventor: Godtfred Kirk Christiansen

This invention relates to toy building elements and more particularly to toy building bricks or blocks adapted to be connected together by means of projections extending from the faces of the elements and arranged so as to engage protruding portions of an adjacent element when two such elements are assembled.

The "gerbil shirt" is just one of Brice Belisle's patented inventions. He's also responsible for a device that holds playing cards (3,761,094), a portable pocket urinal (5,235,705), and what appears to be an attaché case that dispenses measured shots of booze (3,438,551), among others.

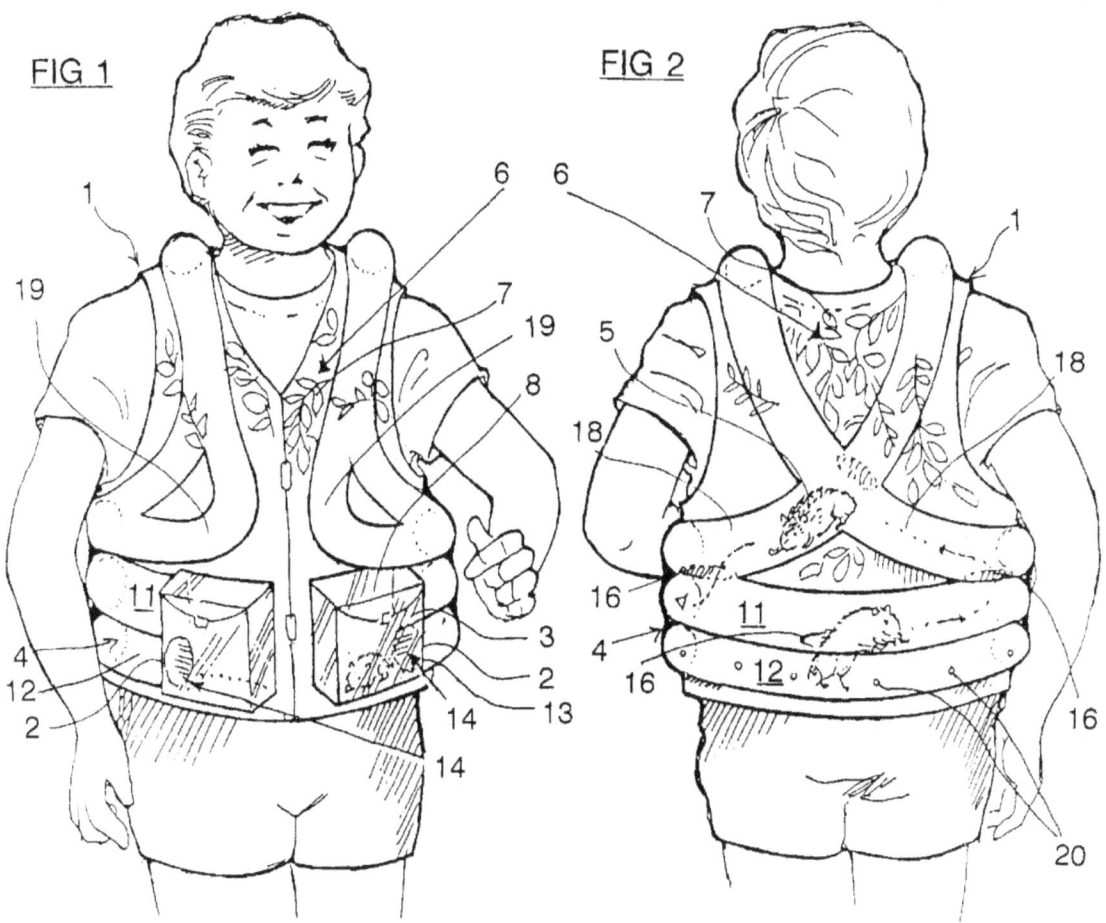

Pet display clothing

U.S. Patent number 5,901,666 (1999)
Inventor: Brice Belisle

A vest or belt is integrally formed with tubular, pet receiving passageways which extend around the wearer's body and terminate in pocket-like chambers for feeding and retrieval. Outer wall portions of the passageways are transparent so that a pet moving along the passageways can be seen by a spectator. Graphics or indicia depicting the pet's habitat or a pet story are marked on the vest and extend across portions of the passageways masking delineations or depicting the passageways as burrows.

The modern whoopee cushion was invented in the 1920s, but it wasn't until much more recently that a self-inflating version became available.

CROSS SECTION - NORMAL INFLATED STATE

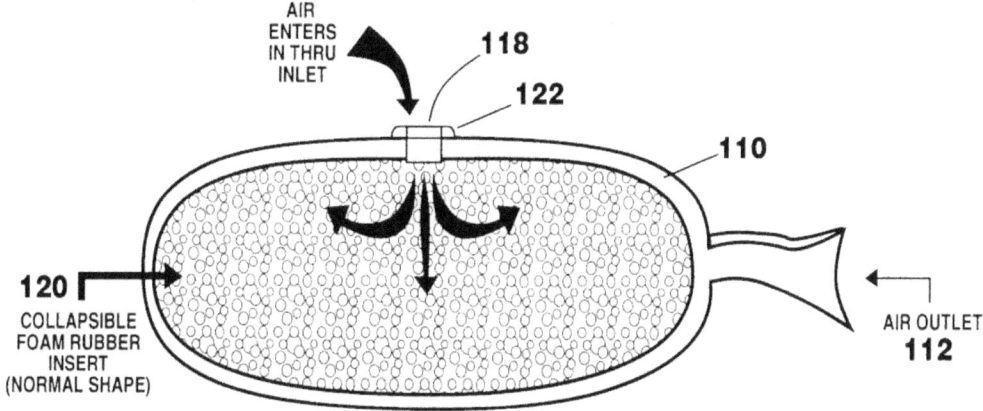

AIR ENTERS IN THRU INLET

118

122

110

120

COLLAPSIBLE FOAM RUBBER INSERT (NORMAL SHAPE)

AIR OUTLET **112**

CROSS SECTION - COMPRESSED STATE

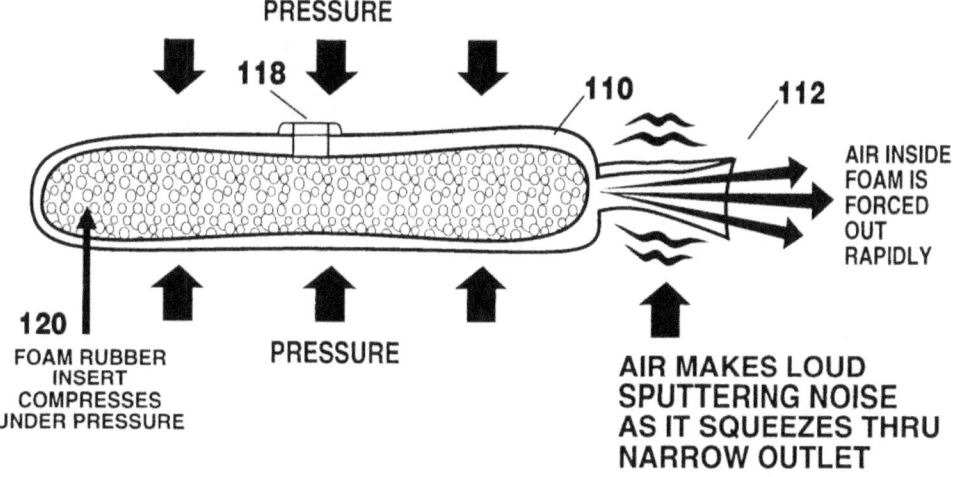

PRESSURE

118

110

112

120

FOAM RUBBER INSERT COMPRESSES UNDER PRESSURE

PRESSURE

AIR INSIDE FOAM IS FORCED OUT RAPIDLY

AIR MAKES LOUD SPUTTERING NOISE AS IT SQUEEZES THRU NARROW OUTLET

Self inflating noise maker

U.S. Patent number 6,331,131 (2001)
Inventor: Russell Morris Selevan

A noise-maker includes an enclosed membrane having an inlet and an outlet that is filled with porous material. The noise-maker is in an inflated state when the porous material is saturated with air and a compressed state when the air is forced out of the porous material. When pressure is applied to the noise-maker, the air inside the membrane is forced through the outlet and the noise-maker reaches the compressed state. When the pressure is released, the noise-maker changes from the compressed state to the inflated state as air flows through the inlet.

Thomas Edison's original phonograph used a grooved cylinder rather than a disc, and his company stuck with the cylinder format until 1929, long after his competitors had switched to discs.

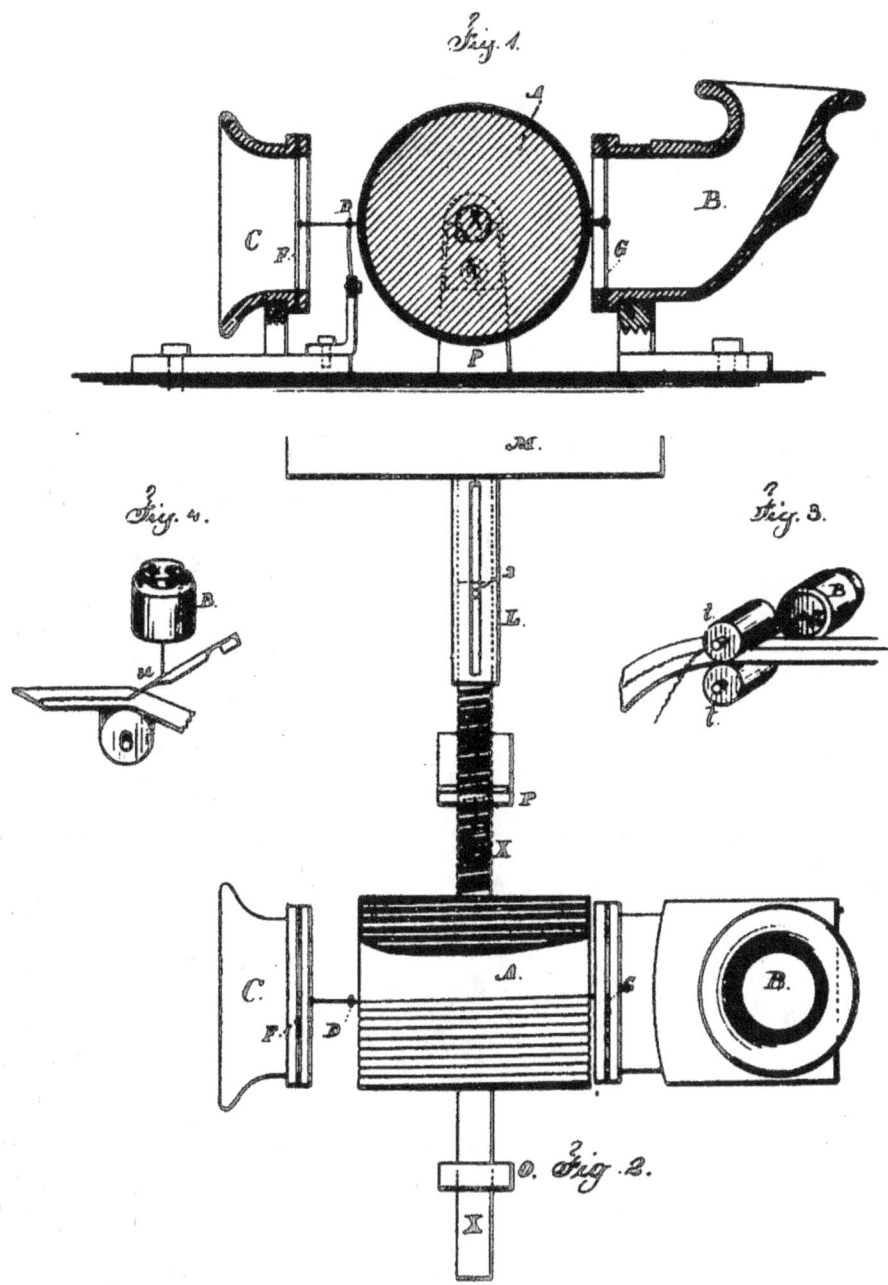

Improvement in phonograph or speaking machines

U.S. Patent number 200,521 (1878)
Inventor: Thomas A. Edison

A noise-maker includes an enclosed membrane having an inlet and an outlet that is filled with porous material. The noise-maker is in an inflated state when the porous material is saturated with air and a compressed state when the air is forced out of the porous material. When pressure is applied to the noise-maker, the air inside the membrane is forced through the outlet and the noise-maker reaches the compressed state. When the pressure is released, the noise-maker changes from the compressed state to the inflated state as air flows through the inlet.

One wonders whether Jamie Lee Curtis's diaper-wiper combo is available in adult sizes, for those times when you've enjoyed just a little too much Activia.

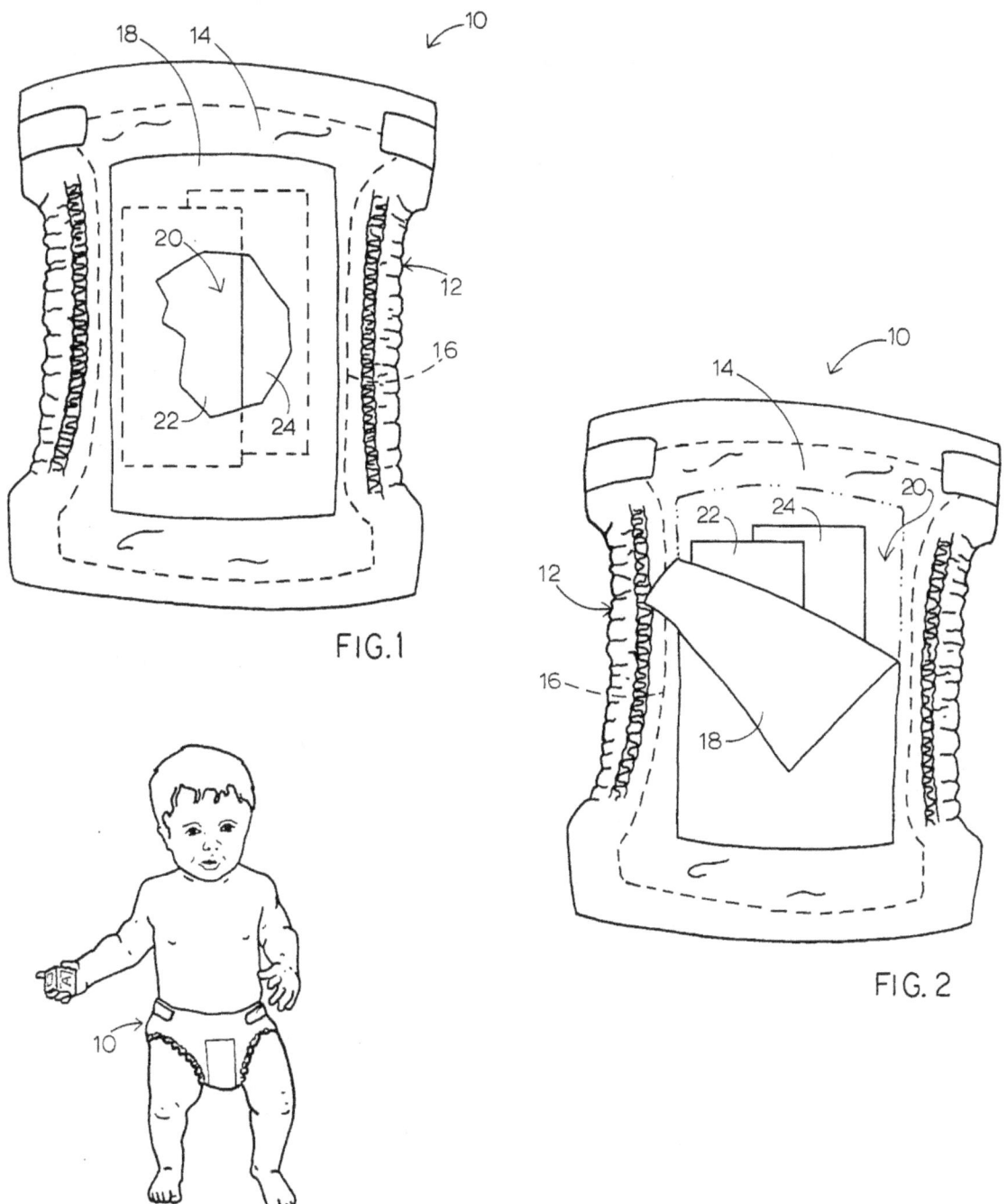

FIG.1

FIG. 2

FIG.3

Infant garment

U.S. Patent number 4,753,647 (1988)
Inventor: Jamie L. Curtis

A disposable infant garment which takes the form of a diaper including, on its outer side, a sealed, but openable, moisture-proof pocket which contains one or more clean-up wipers.

The Magic 8 Ball was introduced in 1950, and improved versions followed over the years.

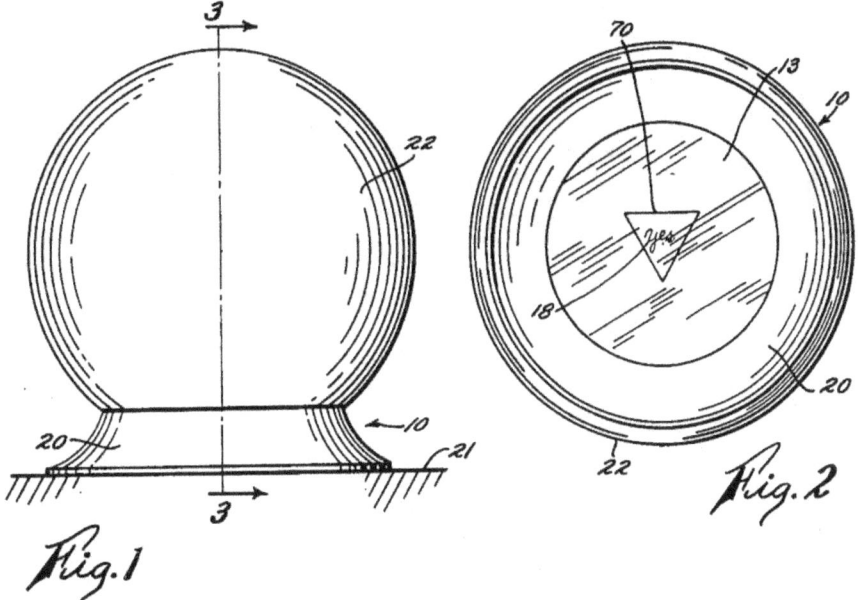

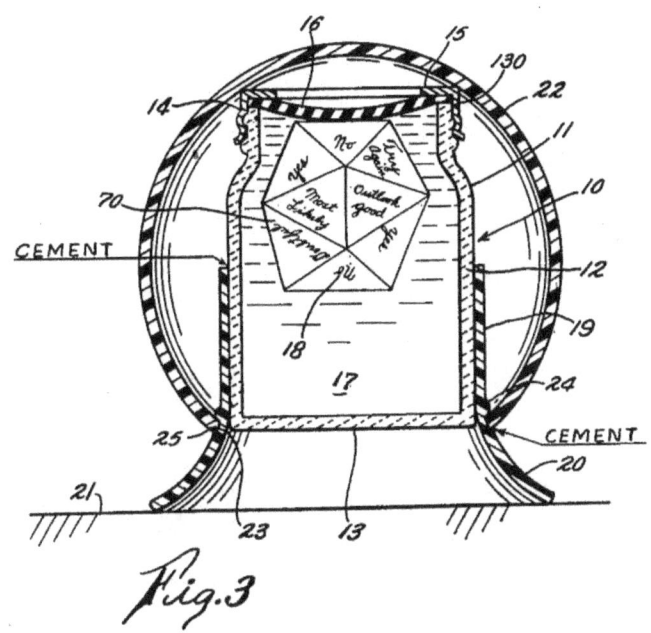

Amusement device

U.S. Patent number 3,168,315 (1965)
Inventor: Abe C. Bookman

This invention relates to improvements in novelty amusement devices and has for its principal objective the construction and co-operation of certain elements thereof to provide for complete protection and effective concealment of device. Another object of the invention is to provide an extremely simplified yet rugged amusement device of the character described that may be fabricated from inexpensive parts in a minimum of manufacturing steps.

The McBee KeySort System was a manual data storage and retrieval technology that used cards with small holes along one or more edges, an edge-notching tool used to remove the paper between a hole and the adjacent edge, and a needle used to retrieve all cards within a stack that did not have a notch at a particular location. McBee cards were commonly used as late as 1980 to organize research data, employee files, library records, and other collections of data. Hypertext developer Douglas Engelbart noted in 1962 that edge-notched cards could be used to implement a hypertext-based information retrieval system.

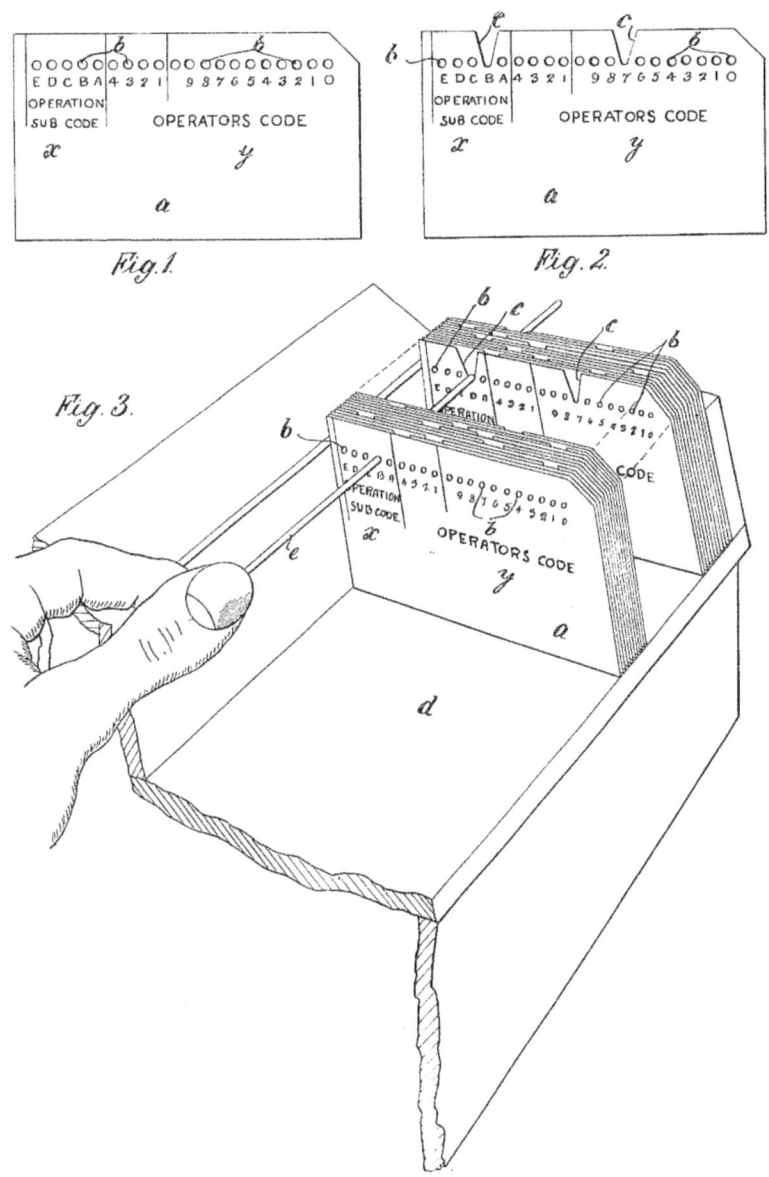

Fig.1.

Fig.2.

Fig.3.

Sorting and classifying of flat sheets, tallies, cards, or the like

U.S. Patent number 1,544,172 (1925)
Inventor: Alfred Perkins

This invention relates to the sorting devices or separating and classifying of flat sheets, tallies, checks, cards or the like of any material, either into numerical or/and alphabetical or other desired order or classification and particularly adapted for use with card indexes, work record cards, election cards, time cards, cost cards or sheets, pay checks, etc. for instance for recording particulars regarding the operatives engaged in a factory, and as examples there may be mentioned the turning up or picking out of single cards from card indexes without the necessity of manual sorting or for the sorting of cards into numerical sequence; in the case of time cards to facilitate putting in correct order in card racks or listing on the pay roll; in the case of record cards for filing purposes; and in the case of work record cards for sorting according to operatives' code number, or again into number order.

The key to Dyson's bladeless Air Multiplier fan, apart from the patented technology, seems to be the fact that anyone who pays over $300 for a fan will rave incessantly about how much better it is than anything else on the market.

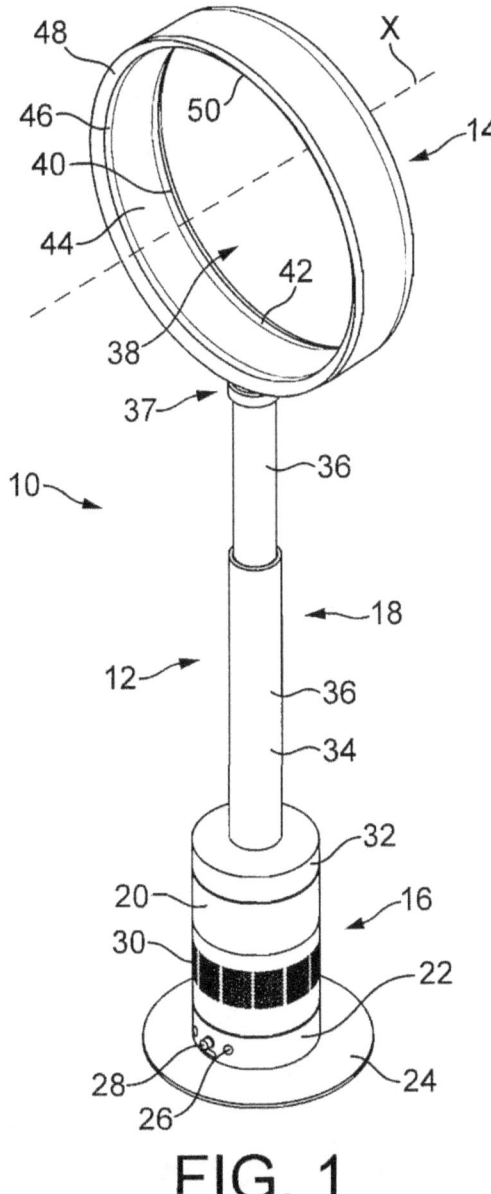

FIG. 1

Fan having a magnetically attached remote control

U.S. Patent number 8,454,322 (2013)
Inventors: Peter David Gammack, James Dyson, Arran George Smith,
Ian John Brough, Mon Shy Teyu, Noorhazelinda Mohd.Salleh

A fan assembly for creating an air current includes an air inlet, an air outlet, an impeller, a motor for rotating the impeller to create an air flow passing from the air inlet to the air outlet, the air outlet comprising an interior passage for receiving the air flow and a mouth for emitting the air flow, the air outlet defining an opening through which air from outside the fan assembly is drawn by the air flow emitted from the mouth, a control circuit for controlling the motor, a remote control for transmitting control signals to the control circuit, and at least one magnet for attaching the remote control to the air outlet.

As the proprietor of one of the most famous brand names in the world, the Coca-Cola Company relies primarily upon trademark law (and, in the case of the formula for its flagship product, trade secret law). But Coca-Cola also holds many patents, including this long-expired design patent for the iconic shape of its bottle.

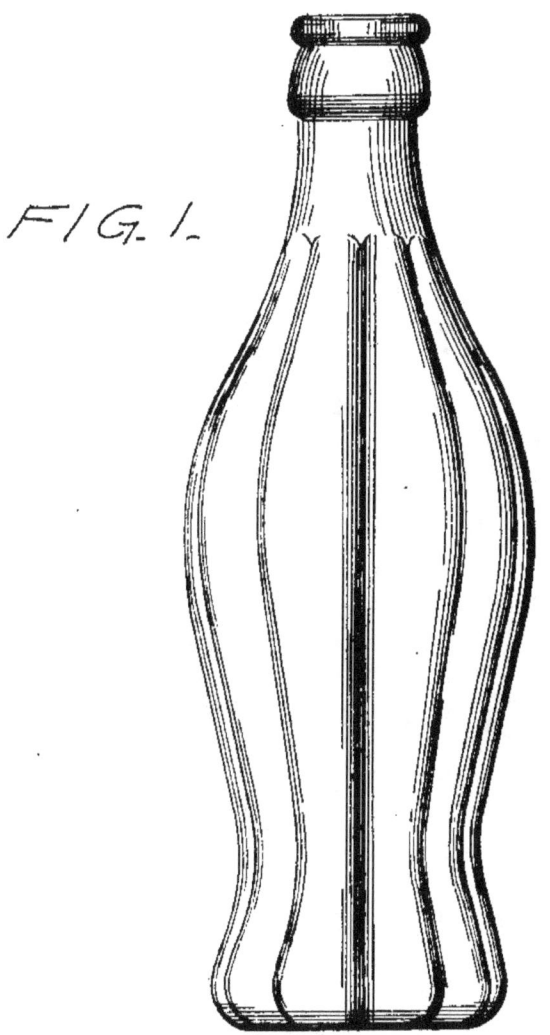

FIG. 1.

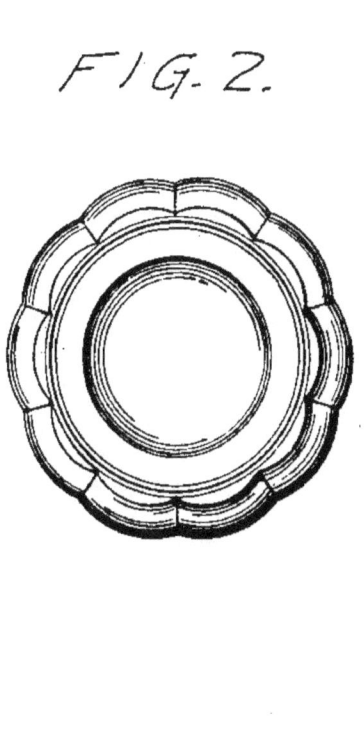

FIG. 2.

Design for a bottle or similar article

U.S. Design Patent number 48,160 (1915)
Inventor: Alexander Samuelson

A new, original, and ornamental Design for Bottles or Similar Articles, of which the following is a specification, reference being had to the accompanying drawings, forming a part thereof. Figure 1 is a perspective view of a bottle showing my design. Fig. 2 is a bottom plan view of the same.

In order to perform a gravity-defying dance move in his live concerts, Michael Jackson and his co-inventors developed a special shoe that enabled him to lean forward 45 degrees without falling.

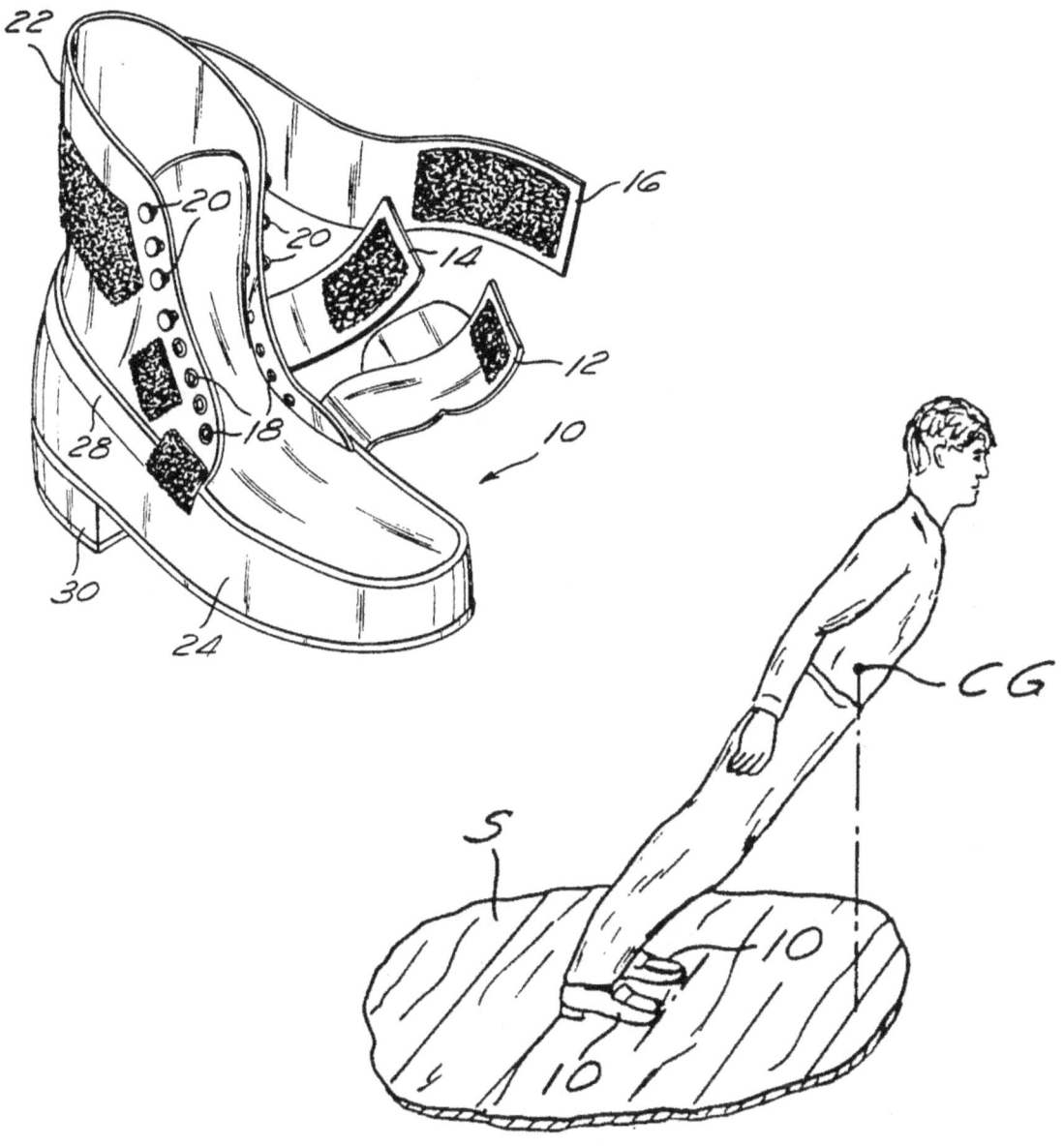

Method and means for creating anti-gravity illusion

U.S. Patent number 5,255,452 (1993)
Inventors: Michael J. Jackson, Michael L. Bush, Dennis Tompkins

A system for allowing a shoe wearer to lean forwardly beyond his center of gravity by virtue of wearing a specially designed pair of shoes which will engage with a hitch member movably projectable through a stage surface. The shoes have a specially designed heel slot which can be detachably engaged with the hitch member by simply sliding the shoe wearer's foot forward, thereby engaging with the hitch member.

www.ingramcontent.com/pod-product-compliance
Lightning Source LLC
Chambersburg PA
CBHW081614170526
45166CB00009B/2966